The Elements of Input-Output Analysis

The Elements of
Input-Output Analysis

by WILLIAM H. MIERNYK

Director, Regional Research Institute, West Virginia University

 Random House / New York

98

Preface

When Wassily Leontief published his "Quantitative Input-Output Relations in the Economic System of the United States" in *The Review of Economics and Statistics* (August 1936), he launched a quiet revolution in economic analysis that has steadily gained momentum. That the article, which represents a turning point in the development of economic thought, did not at first attract wide attention was partly a matter of timing. The nations of the free world were in the midst of the Great Depression. And John Maynard Keynes had just published his *General Theory of Employment, Interest, and Money,* a treatise that immediately attracted worldwide attention since it was focused on the problem of chronic unemployment in the capitalist economies of that day.

Unlike Keynes, Leontief was not concerned with the causes of disequilibrium in a particular type of economic system during a particular phase of its development. He was interested in the *structure* of economic systems, in the way the component parts of an economy fit together and influence one another. Leontief fashioned an analytical model that can be applied to any kind of economic system during any phase of its development. As he himself noted, input-output analysis is above all an analytical *tool.* It can be used in the analysis of a wide variety of economic problems, and as a guide for the implementation of various kinds of economic policies.

Input-output analysis is a branch of econometrics, and the technical literature in the field draws heavily on the arcana of mathematics. For the beginning student of economics, and perhaps even for some professional economists, the mathematical nature of the literature has been a barrier. The present book covers the essentials of input-output analysis entirely in non-mathematical terms, although a certain amount of arithmetic is used to illustrate various steps in the analysis. For those who are interested, the last chapter includes a description of the model in elementary mathematical terms and the rudiments of matrix algebra needed to understand the description. The final chapter is largely independent of the remainder of the book — it can be read first or last, or it can be ignored entirely if one is content to accept some of the conclusions reached in earlier chapters without a mathematical demonstration.

It should be emphasized that this volume deals with input-output *analysis* rather than with the statistical problems involved in the construction of an input-output table. It is designed to give the reader an understanding of how the input-output system works; it is not a guide to the construction of an interindustry transactions table.

Most of this book deals with a static, open input-output model. This is the model upon which the 1947 tables for the United States were based. These tables were published by the Bureau of Labor Statistics of the U. S. Department of Labor and have been described in detail by W. Duane Evans and Marvin Hoffenberg in "The Interindustry Relations Study for 1947," *The Review of Economics and Statistics* (May 1952). A more recent input-output study, based on 1958 data, has been completed by the Office of Business Economics of the U. S. Department of Commerce. A report on this study has been published by Morris R. Goldman, Martin L. Marimont, and Beatrice N. Vaccara in "The Interindustry Structure of the United States," *Survey of Current Business* (November 1964). The major difference between the 1947 and 1958 studies is that the latter has been integrated, both conceptually and statistically, with the national income and product accounts regularly published by the U. S. Department of Commerce.

The present volume is a complete revision and a substantial expansion of my earlier *Primer of Input-Output Economics* published by the Bureau of Business and Economic Research, Northeastern University, in 1957. I am grateful to the administration of Northeastern University for permission to use copyrighted material from this publication. Thanks are also due the

Harvard University Press for permission to reproduce an illustrative table from the November 1951 issue of the *Review of Economics and Statistics*.

Parts of an earlier draft were read by Professors Walter Isard of the University of Pennsylvania, Charles M. Tiebout, of the University of Washington, and David Rearick, a former colleague at the University of Colorado. I am grateful for their helpful and encouraging comments. The entire manuscript of the earlier draft was read by Professor William Letwin of M.I.T. and by two of my graduate research assistants, Mr. John H. Chapman, Jr., and Mr. Kenneth Shellhammer. I wish to thank them for a number of helpful editorial and substantive suggestions. Finally, it is a pleasure to acknowledge the efficient secretarial services provided by Mrs. Mig Shepherd and Mrs. Suzanne Roberts. Needless to say, I alone am responsible for any errors or omissions that remain.

Boulder, Colorado   WILLIAM H. MIERNYK
January, 1965

Contents

The Elements of Input-Output Analysis

1 Introduction

Approaches to Economic Analysis

The first writers to treat economics systematically — Adam Smith and his immediate successors — dealt with the economy as a whole. In today's terminology they were concerned with *macro*economics. Later economists, notably Alfred Marshall and his followers in the Neo-classical school, focused upon the household and the firm. They inaugurated the era of *micro*economics which led to Chamberlin's theory of monopolistic competition and Mrs. Robinson's theory of imperfect competition. The Neo-classical economists and their successors analyzed the forces which result in economic equilibrium, but their approach was that of *partial* equilibrium, or the method of examining "one thing at a time."

During the 1930s, under the influence of John Maynard Keynes, there was a revival of interest in aggregative economics. Keynesians drew on the work of both Classical and Neo-classical schools. Like the latter, they were concerned with the forces which result in equilibrium or disequilibrium, but they returned to the Classical tradition in their emphasis on the economy as a whole. The Neo-classical economists had devoted much of their attention to the theory of value — examination of the forces which determine prices under given market conditions. The Keynesians, however, were primarily concerned with the determinants of income and employment. Their system was based on broad aggregates: total employment, total consumption, total investment, and national income. Keynesian economists showed how these variables are related to one another, and how changes in one affect the rest. They were much less interested than the Neo-classical economists in examining the effects of a change in one variable on the assumption that all others remained fixed. In this sense the Keynesians were concerned with *general* rather than partial equilibrium. But neither the Neo-classical economists nor the Keynesians were directly concerned with *economic interdependence,* with the *structure* of the economy and the way in which its individual sectors fit together.

Economic Interdependence

There were departures from the developments of economic thought discussed in the preceding section, and some of these came quite early. In 1758, for example, François Quesnay published his *Tableau Economique,* a device which stressed the *interdependence of economic activities.* Quesnay's original *Tableau* depicted the operation of a single establishment, a farm. It showed graphically the successive "rounds" of wealth-producing activity which resulted from a given increment in output. In this sense it was a forerunner of modern multiplier analysis. Later Quesnay published a modified version of the *Tableau* which represented the entire economy of his day in the form of circular flows. While this is an interesting early attempt at macroeconomic *analysis,* the notion of interdependence is better expressed in his earlier version.[1]

The next link in this chain of development did not come for more than a century. In 1874, Léon Walras published his *Éléments d'économie politique pure.* Walras, like other economists of his time, was largely concerned with the question of price determination. Unlike his contemporaries, however, he was interested in the *simultaneous* determination of all prices in the economy. His model consisted of a system of equations — one for each price to be determined. Thus he made the transition from partial to *general* equilibrium.

---

[1] For an excellent discussion of Quesnay's work, with illustrations, see Philip Charles Newman, *The Development of Economic Thought* (Englewood Cliffs, N.J.: Prentice-Hall, Inc., 1952), pp. 34–40. An ingenious translation of Quesnay's *Tableau* into an input-output model is given by Almarin Phillips in "The *Tableau Economique* as a Simple Leontief Model," *Quarterly Journal of Economics,* LXIX (February 1955), 137–44, reprinted in James A. Gherity, *Economic Thought, A Historical Anthology* (New York: Random House, 1965), pp. 150–58.

Walras' interest was not limited to the general equilibrium of exchange, however; he was also interested in the general equilibrium of *production*. In his theory of production Walras made use of "coefficients of production." These were determined, in his view, by technology, and they measured the quantities of factors required to produce a unit of each kind of finished goods. Thus in the Walrasian system *all* prices are determined — those of the factors of production as well as the prices of finished goods.[2]

The model developed by Walras shows interdependence among the producing sectors of the economy, and the competing demands of each sector for the factors of production. His system also includes equations representing consumer income and expenditure, and it allows consumers to substitute the products of one sector for those produced by others. It also takes into account costs of production in each sector, the total demand for and supply of commodities, and the demand for and supply of factors of production.

Walras, who was a skilled mathematician, considered his system a purely theoretical model. He believed that even if the data were available to implement his model, the computational problems would be formidable if not insurmountable. This view is understandable since only rudimentary statistics were available at the time Walras wrote, and he could not, of course, foresee the development of high-speed digital computers which are now able to handle much more complex systems than the one Walras developed.

Other economists — notably Gustav Cassel of Sweden and Vilfredo Pareto of Italy — contributed to the theory of general equilibrium. But the culmination of the work started by Quesnay came in the 1930s when Professor Wassily Leontief of Harvard developed a general theory of production based on the notion of economic interdependence. An equally important contribution was made by Leontief when he gave his theory empirical content and published the first input-output table for the American economy.[3]

[2] See "Hicks on Walras," in Henry William Spiegel (ed.), *The Development of Economic Thought* (New York: John Wiley & Sons, Inc., 1952), pp. 581–91.

[3] Leontief's basic ideas were first published in his article "Quantitative Input-Output Relations in the Economic System of the United States," *The Review of Economics and Statistics,* XVIII (August 1936), 105–25. These ideas were

Leontief's original table showed how each sector of the economy depended upon every other sector, but it was still highly aggregated. The subsequent development of high-speed electronic computers—and of efficient computational methods—permitted a great deal of disaggregation. Large tables have since been published representing the economy in considerable detail.

Input-output or interindustry analysis is an important branch of economics today. The input-output method has spread rapidly throughout the world. Input-output tables have been prepared for at least forty national economies, and the number of regional and small-area input-output tables has grown at a rapid rate.

The input-output method is widely used as an analytical tool in highly developed economies—both those which engage in economic planning and those which rely primarily on the market mechanism for the allocation of resources and distribution of income. More recently, a number of underdeveloped nations have turned to this new and powerful technique as a guide to important policy decisions.

As indicated above, not all input-output studies are conducted at the level of the national economy. In the United States, in particular, there has been a rapid growth of small-area input-output studies. Some models deal with a single region, but others are interregional in character. Some deal with single communities; others compare a number of communities. Some are primarily concerned with a single sector, such as agriculture or mining, but others are small-scale versions of the national models.

Where does input-output analysis fit within the larger body of economics? Broadly, it is part of economic statistics. More precisely, however, it is part of econometrics—that branch of economics which is a blend of theoretical, mathematical, and statistical analysis. Most of the literature dealing with this

expanded in other journal articles, and in 1941 Leontief's first book on input-output economics was published under the title *The Structure of American Economy, 1919–1929*. An expanded version of this book, covering the period 1919–1939, was published by Oxford University Press in 1951. The results of more recent research, including a discussion of dynamic and regional input-output models, are presented in Wassily Leontief and others, *Studies in the Structure of the American Economy* (New York: Oxford University Press, 1953). For a comprehensive list of other contributions through 1963, see Charlotte E. Taskier, *Input-Output Bibliography, 1955–1960* (New York: United Nations, 1961), and *Input-Output Bibliography, 1960–1963* (New York: United Nations, 1964).

relatively young field is couched in abstract mathematical language. Simplified expositions dealing with part of the technique — usually a basic transactions table — have become fairly common. But the student who is interested in a comprehensive introduction to the subject has to wade through rigorous mathematical formulations.

The purpose of this volume is to present a nonmathematical exposition of the input-output system using a highly simplified illustrative example. A large input-output table, or matrix, is quite complicated, and not ideally suited for classroom discussion. On the assumption that it will be easier to teach the fundamentals of this method by a simpler approach, an abbreviated and simplified hypothetical input-output table has been constructed. The meaning of this table is easier to explain than that of the larger tables which have been published. The hypothetical values inserted in the table may not be realistic (since small numbers were selected to facilitate exposition), but in other respects the table is an accurate representation of an actual input-output matrix. The reader who learns to follow the directions given for this hypothetical table can easily turn to an actual table and understand its meaning without further instruction. For those who wish to go on, an introduction to the rudiments of the mathematics used in input-output analysis is given in Chapter 7; concise symbolic formulation is also included in that chapter. With this background, the student can proceed to more technical treatments such as those given by Chenery and Clark in their estimable *Interindustry Economics,*[4] the basic works published by Leontief and his associates, and the excellent and detailed description by Evans and Hoffenberg[5] of how an input-output table is put together.

The following chapter deals with the transactions table — the basis of all input-output analysis — and the coefficients which are derived from this table. Later chapters cover more specialized topics, including the application of the input-output method to a variety of economic problems.

[4] Hollis B. Chenery and Paul G. Clark, *Interindustry Economics* (New York: John Wiley & Sons, Inc., 1959).
[5] W. Duane Evans and Marvin Hoffenberg, "The Interindustry Relations Study for 1947," *The Review of Economics and Statistics,* XXXIV (May 1952), 97–142.

2 Input-Output Analysis

The basis of Leontief's analytical system is the input-output table. This table shows how the output of each industry is distributed among other industries and sectors of the economy. At the same time it shows the *inputs* to each industry from other industries and sectors. A hypothetical input-output or *transactions* table is illustrated by Table 2–1. This table, which appears on page 9, will be referred to frequently in the chapters to follow and has therefore also been reproduced on a tear-out page at the back of the book. (The same applies to Tables 2–2 and 2–3.) The illustrative table is highly simplified, in that only six hypothetical industries are included, but it is realistic in other respects. An actual input-output table may include from 50 to 200 industries, depending upon the degree of aggregation desired. Data were collected by the Bureau of Labor Statistics to make up a 500-industry table in the 1947 study, although the table itself was not published.

Some advantage is gained by disaggregation; that is, by having a detailed breakdown of industries and sectors. If an input-output table is to be used for forecasting, for example, a detailed industrial classification would reveal where bottlenecks might occur during the expansion of production. There are times, however, when it is useful to consolidate the sectors of a large table into a more compact table.[1] This is the case when attention is to be focused on one or two particular sectors. As a general rule, however, input-output analysts strive for the maximum amount of disaggregation when constructing a basic transactions table.

[1] This leads to a number of statistical problems, however, and treatment of these problems is outside the scope of an introduction to input-output analysis. For a discussion of this aspect of the aggregation problem see Walter D. Fisher, "Criteria for Aggregation in Input-Output Analysis," *The Review of Economics and Statistics,* XL (August 1958), 250–60.

TABLE 2-1
Hypothetical Transactions Table*
Industry Purchasing

		Processing Sector						Final Demand					
Inputs² \ Outputs¹		(1) A	(2) B	(3) C	(4) D	(5) E	(6) F	(7) Gross inventory accumulation (+)	(8) Exports to foreign countries	(9) Government purchases	(10) Gross private capital formation	(11) Households	(12) Total Gross Output
(1) Industry A		10	15	1	2	5	6	2	5	1	3	14	64
(2) Industry B		5	4	7	1	3	8	1	6	3	4	17	59
(3) Industry C		7	2	8	1	5	3	2	3	1	3	5	40
(4) Industry D		11	1	2	8	6	4	0	0	1	2	4	39
(5) Industry E		4	0	1	14	3	2	1	2	1	3	9	40
(6) Industry F		2	6	7	6	2	6	2	4	2	1	8	46
(7) Gross inventory depletion (−)		1	2	1	0	2	1	0	1	0	0	0	8
(8) Imports		2	1	3	0	3	2	0	0	0	0	2	13
(9) Payments to government		2	3	2	2	1	2	3	2	1	2	12	32
(10) Depreciation allowances		1	2	1	0	1	0	0	0	0	0	0	5
(11) Households		19	23	7	5	9	12	1	0	8	0	1	85
(12) Total Gross Outlays		64	59	40	39	40	46	12	23	18	18	72	431

Industry Producing
Payments Sector   Processing Sector

¹Sales to industries and sectors along the top of the table from the industry listed in each row at the left of the table.
²Purchases from industries and sectors at the left of the table by the industry listed at the top of each column.
*This table has been reproduced on a tear-out sheet at the back of the book.

It has been customary in the United States, and in most other countries as well, to value transactions in terms of *producers' prices*. Also, in the case of trade activities, outputs are defined as "gross margins" rather than the total value of all transactions — that is, the value of goods handled by trade establishments is not counted. There are a number of technical problems involved in the measurement of gross margins which cannot be discussed here.[2] For present purposes it will be convenient to view gross margins as a "mark-up" on the goods handled by trade establishments as a payment for the creation of time-and-place utility.

A prodigious amount of labor is required to construct an input-output table, but once made up it is fairly easy to "read" or interpret. If the reader has no difficulty in understanding the small hypothetical table considered here he will have no difficulty in interpreting the much larger tables that have been published. We will trace through a series of transactions to show the inner workings of the table, but first we will explain its various parts.

Assume that the transactions recorded in the table are in billions of dollars. Each *row* (reading from left to right) shows the output sold by each industry or sector along the left-hand side of the table to each industry or sector across the top of the table. Each column (reading from top to bottom) shows the purchases made by each industry or sector along the top of the table from the industries and sectors along the left-hand side. Since this is a square table, there is one row to correspond to each column.

To illustrate, consider the relationship between industry E (row 5 and column 5) and industry C (row 3 and column 3). To find the share of industry E's output sold to industry C, read *across* row 5 until it intersects column 3. We see that industry E sold one billion dollars' worth of goods to industry C during the period covered by the table. To find how much industry E *buys from* industry C, go over to column 5 and read down until this column intersects row 3. We see that industry E *bought from*

[2]For a discussion of this and other statistical problems involved in the construction of a transactions table see W. Duane Evans and Marvin Hoffenberg, "The Interindustry Relations Study for 1947," *The Review of Economics and Statistics*, XXXIV (May 1952), 97–142. See also *The 1947 Interindustry Relations Study, Industry Reports: General Explanations*, U. S. Department of Labor, Bureau of Labor Statistics, Report No. 9 (March 1953) and *Industry Reports: Manufacturing Methodology*, BLS Report No. 10, *idem* (March 1953).

industry C products worth five billion dollars. Hence the *net* transaction between industries C and E during this period is four billion dollars in *favor* of industry C. There is nothing difficult about reading the table provided we remember the following simple rules:

1. To find the amount of purchases from one industry by another, locate the *purchasing industry* at the top of the table, then read *down the column* until you come to the *producing industry*.
2. To find the amount of sales from one industry to another, locate the *selling industry* along the left side of the table, then read *across* the row until you come to the *buying industry*.

The Make-up of the Table

1. *The Processing Sector.* The upper left-hand corner of the table has been set off in heavy double lines and labeled the processing sector. This is the sector of an input-output table which contains the industries producing goods and services. Among them we would find agriculture, various manufacturing industries, transportation, communications and other utilities, wholesale and retail trade, the service industries, construction, and as many other industries as are isolated for separate treatment in the table. This is the portion of the hypothetical table that is highly simplified, and in practice we would expect to find this sector expanded to 50 or more industries, thus greatly expanding the size of the entire table.

2. *The Payments Sector.* On the left-hand side of the table, rows 7 to 11 are set off under the heading *payments sector*. This sector includes these five rows *read all the way across the table.* We shall examine each of the five parts of the payments sector in turn.

a. Row 7, *gross inventory depletion.* By gross inventory depletion we mean the using up of previously accumulated stocks of raw materials, intermediate goods, or finished products. Thus in row 7, column 2, we see that during the period covered by the table industry B used up two billion dollars' worth of the stock it had put into inventory in an earlier period. The amount of inventory depletion in all other industries and sectors can be found by reading down each column until it intersects row 7.

b. Row 8, *imports.* To find the value of imports purchased by each industry and sector, read down each column until it comes to row 8. This procedure shows, for example, that industry E imported three billion dollars' worth of goods from abroad, while industry D imported nothing.

c. Row 9, *payments to government.* For simplicity, assume that payments to governments (federal, state, and local) in the form of taxes, represent purchases of government services such as police and fire protection, maintenance of the armed forces, and similar services which most of us take for granted. Although there is no direct correspondence between payments to government and the amount of government services provided to each industry (because, for example, how do you "value" the protection of the Army and Navy?), it will simplify matters if we assume that the figures in row 9 represent the value of government services to each of the industries and other sectors listed across the top of the table.

d. Row 10, *depreciation allowances.* Reading across row 10 we see the amounts of depreciation allowances set aside by each of the industries listed across the top of the table. These numbers approximate the cost of plant and equipment used up in the production of the goods represented in this table. Note, for example, that industry A (column 1) allowed one billion dollars during the period covered by the table for the depreciation of machinery and other equipment.[3]

e. Row 11, *households.* This row represents the wages, salaries, dividends, interest, and similar payments made to households by each of the industries and other sectors listed across the top of the table. We have inserted fairly large figures in this row to indicate in particular the relative importance of payments to labor in our hypothetical economy. Industry A paid out 19 billion dollars in the form of wages, salaries, and other forms of house-

---

[3] An input-output table is compiled for a given time period. In practice this is usually a calendar year. There is no reason, however, why the period could not be either longer or shorter than a year.

hold income; industry B paid out 23 billion dollars, and so on across row 11.

3. *The Final Demand Sector.* The final demand sector consists of columns 7 through 11 *read all the way down the table.* The final demand sector is of special importance because it is the *autonomous* sector — the one in which changes occur which are transmitted throughout the rest of the table. It is here that the transactions which will be discussed presently originate. We will describe each of the parts of this sector briefly.

a. Column 7, *gross inventory accumulation.* This column shows the amounts of *additions* to inventories held by each of the industries and sectors along the left-hand side of the table. During any given time period some of the goods produced do not get into the hands of their final consumers. Retailers must stand ready to provide consumers with a variety of goods at all times. Hence they must keep a stock of goods on their shelves. Wholesalers must likewise be ready to ship to retailers upon short notice. And manufacturers will usually have a stock of the goods they produce on hand at any given time. Column 7 shows the amounts of inventories accumulated during the period covered by the table *regardless of where those inventories are held,* whether at the factory, in warehouses, or in retail establishments.

b. Column 8, *exports.* This column shows the value of exports from each of the processing industries and other sectors during the period covered by the table. Note that industry A in our hypothetical economy exported five billion dollars' worth of goods while households exported nothing. This would be typical of a national table since residents of one country ordinarily do not sell their labor services in another country. In regional applications, however, households can export labor services across regional boundaries, and it is also fairly common for management and technical consulting services to be exported from one region to another.

c. Column 9, *government purchases.* Purchases made by all levels of government are given in this column. The entry where the government column and the government row intersect indicates that there are some intragovernmental transactions, just as there are transactions within other industries and sectors included in our table.

d. Column 10, *gross private capital formation.* This column shows the amount of sales from each industry or sector along the left side of the table to buyers who use their purchases for private capital formation. All entries in the transactions table, except those in column 10, are on *current* account. Purchases *by all buyers* for the replacement of or additions to plant and equipment — and any other purchases which are entered on *capital* account — are summarized by the entries in column 10. Viewed another way, each entry in column 10 can be considered an input from the industry or sector listed at the left to the Gross Private Capital Formation "industry."

e. Column 11, *households.* The entries in this column represent purchases of finished goods and services by their ultimate consumers from the industries and other sectors along the left-hand side of the table.

4. *Total Gross Output and Total Gross Outlay.* The final row and the final column of the table have yet to be explained.

Row 12, *total gross outlay,* shows the total value of *inputs* to each of the industries and sectors in each column at the top of the table. The total value of *purchases* by industry A, for example, is 64 billion dollars, the amount of the entry in row 12, column 1.

The input-output table is essentially a system of double-entry bookkeeping. Within each industry in the processing sector all of the receipts from sales are paid out for goods and services purchased from other industries or sectors. It might help to think of these as payments to factors of production. Some of the receipts are paid to the government in taxes, and some might be added to capital account. But the receipts from all outputs will just balance total outlays for each industry. After taking into account appropriate inventory changes, *the total gross output,* column 12, of each industry in the processing sector is equal to the total outlays made by that industry. Thus in the hypothetical table, the first six entries in the Total Gross Output column are identical with the first six entries in the Total Gross Outlay row.

This is not true of the totals in the remaining rows and columns, however. We would not expect imports and exports to be exactly equal in any given year. Nor are inventory depletions and inventory accumulations likely to be the same during a given time period. Similarly, one would not expect a balance between government purchases and payments to governments, capital spending and depreciation allowances, and payments to and by households in the same year. But the individual differences must "cancel out" when we view the entire economy. As is true of any single processing industry, *total* outlays must equal *total* outputs for the economy as a whole. The total of all rows in the payments sector must equal the total of all columns in the final demand sector for the same reason that the Gross National Product computed from the product side must equal Gross National Product computed from factor payments.

One last point may be raised before tracing through a set of transactions. How does the Total Gross Output (or Total Gross Outlay) in the input-output table compare with Gross National Product? They are not the same. The GNP is defined as "the current market value of final goods and services produced in a given year." But even for the same year, GNP will not be the same as the Total Gross Output of an input-output table. *In computing GNP every effort is made to eliminate double-counting.* But since the input-output table measures *all transactions* in the economy the value of goods and services produced in a given year is counted more than one time; that is, we deliberately *double-count.*

The objective is different in the two cases. In national-income analysis the object is to measure the final value of goods and services produced by the entire economy in a given year. We obviously wish to count one time only each good and service produced. In the input-output table, however, we wish to account for all *transactions.* Since some goods will enter into more than one transaction, their value must be counted each time a different transaction takes place. What we have then is an accumulation of value added at each stage of the production process until a good gets into the hands of its final consumer.

Input-output analysis and national-income accounting are not two separate branches of economics, however. As noted in the preface, the 1958 table for the United States has been completely reconciled with our national income and product accounts.

There is nothing rigid about the classifications used in the payments and final demand sectors of the hypothetical transactions table. The industries in the processing sector can be disaggregated to any degree desired — within the limits of data availability. Similarly, the payments and final demand sectors can be split into more rows and columns than those shown in Table 2–1. For example, the import row (and export column) can be disaggregated along geographic lines. Instead of a single government row (and column) there can be three, one each for federal, state, and local governments. And the household row (and column) could be further divided; for example, on the basis of income distribution. The input-output table is a flexible analytical tool. It can be made as detailed or as condensed as necessary for any given purpose. The only limitation is that there must be one row for each column in the processing sector. It is convenient, although not necessary, to have a final demand column for each row in the payments sector.

There is no fixed rule for including (or excluding) any specific economic activity in the final demand (or payments) sector. Table 2–1 illustrates a relatively "open" input-output model. For some purposes it might be desirable to "close" the system with respect to one or more of the activities in the final demand (payments) sector. Households, for example, can be shifted into the processing sector, and the same is true of any other activity in final demand.[4] Similarly, some activities normally included in the processing sector can be shifted to final demand. The construction and maintenance industry can be included in final demand, for example, if one is interested in analyzing the interindustry effects of changes in construction activity. The decision of how "open" or "closed" an input-output table is to be depends largely upon the purpose for which it is to be used. Our hypothetical example illustrates a general-purpose, open, nondynamic input-output system. But it must be emphasized that the basic model can be altered in a number of ways, depending upon the analytical use for which it is intended.

Tracing through a Set of Transactions

Let us now trace through a set of transactions involving one of the hypothetical industries in the processing sector of the input-

---

[4] An illustration is given in Chapter 3.

output table. Consider the sales made by industry C, and the purchases made by the same industry.

The output side. A look at the transactions table indicates that industry C sold seven billion dollars' worth of goods to industry A during the period covered by the table, and it sold two billion dollars' worth to industry B. *Intraindustry transactions* amounted to eight billion dollars. This means that the firms in industry C purchased from each other goods valued at this amount. Other sales to industries D, E, and F came to one, five, and three billion dollars respectively. This accounts for all transactions within the processing sector of the table.

Additions to inventory in industry C were valued at two billion dollars during the period, and this industry exported three billion dollars' worth of goods to foreign countries. It sold one billion dollars' worth of goods to various government agencies. During the period covered by the table a total of five billion dollars was spent on the finished products of industry C by households. And three billion dollars' worth of the output of this industry was used by its buyers for replacement of or additions to capital equipment. Altogether, the total gross output of industry C was valued at 40 billion dollars in our hypothetical economy.

The input side. Let us look at the purchases made by industry C from the other industries in the table. Purchases from industry A amounted to one billion dollars; from B, seven billion; from D, two billion; and from E and F, one and seven billion respectively. Industry C also used up inventories amounting to one billion, and imported three billion dollars' worth of goods from other countries. It paid taxes of two billion, and set aside one billion in depreciation allowances. Finally, the industry paid out seven billion dollars in wages and salaries. Once again, these individual items must add up to 40 billion dollars – the amount entered in the Total Gross Outlay row.

The interested reader can repeat this process for any industry or sector shown in the table. He will soon develop a facility for following through a set of transactions.

Industries and Sectors

A transactions table consists of a collection of industries and sectors, and it might be helpful to distinguish between these concepts. According to Tiebout, "industries refer to aggregates of firms producing similar products. Sectors refer to the kinds of markets that industries serve."[5] This is a useful distinction to keep in mind. When discussing the transactions table, however, we have at times referred to one collection of activities as the processing sector, and we have spoken of the individual activities outside this category as *the* final demand sector when they are considered collectively. Thus the term *sector* may be used at times with slightly different meanings, but the meaning which applies in each case should be clear from the context of the discussion.

All firms engaged in producing similar goods, or providing similar services, make up an *industry*. The concept of the industry is a fuzzy one because of the problem of overlapping. Not many large manufacturing firms, for example, make one product only. The same firm may manufacture automobiles, tractors, refrigerators, deep-freeze units, television sets, and perhaps a wide variety of other products. Generally, however, a firm is classified on the basis of its *principal product*. If this firm is engaged primarily in the manufacture of automobiles it is included in the automobile industry. If we are interested in analyzing the refrigerator industry, however, we must include in the industry that portion of this firm's activities devoted to the production of refrigerators. A useful method for solving the problem of overlapping in defining an industry has been developed by P. Sargent Florence.[6]

Consider, for example, the case of four firms manufacturing three products. We will label the firms A, B, C, and D, and the products x, y, and z. The firms may be classified into industries X, Y, and Z. If we arrange the firms and their products as shown in Figure 2–1 we can easily see the principal product of each firm and this will tell us the industry under which that firm should be classified.

Firm A clearly belongs to industry X although it also manufactures smaller quantities of y and z. Firm B belongs to industry Y, and firm C to industry Z. Firm D also belongs to industry X

[5] Charles M. Tiebout, *The Community Economic Base Study* (New York: Committee for Economic Development, December 1962), p. 29.

[6] *Investment Location, and Size of Plant* (Cambridge: The University Press, 1948), p. 3.

FIGURE 2–1
Product-Mix of Hypothetical Firms

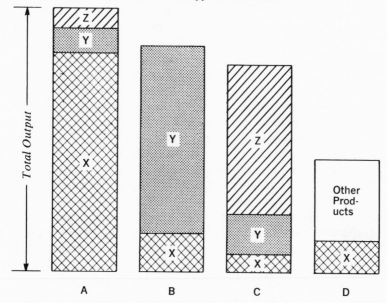

Firms

NOTE: The height of each bar represents
total output; the segments show
the value of each product as a
per cent of total output.

although it makes a wide variety of other products. If we are
interested in measuring the total output of industry X it will be
necessary to go to all four of the above firms, although only two
of them are classified under industry X. The problem of overlapping is primarily a statistical one, encountered when we
attempt to measure employment or production in individual
industries. It need not trouble us at present, however, since we
are only interested in developing the concept of the industry.

   A number of industries, different in some respects but similar
in others, may be considered collectively as an *industry group.*

All of the firms which specialize in the manufacture of cotton yarn, for example, make up one industry; firms which make the yarn into cloth make up another industry; and firms which dye or otherwise finish the cloth make up a third.[7]

A similar distinction may be made in the case of firms specializing in various stages of the production of woolen or synthetic cloth. Each group of firms constitutes a separate industry, but all of them together are members of the *textile industry group*. In 1945 a Standard Industrial Classification was prepared by several government agencies and published by the Bureau of the Budget. According to this classification (abbreviated as SIC) there are 20 major manufacturing industry groups.[8]

The operating unit of American industry is the *establishment*. In general, an establishment consists of a single plant or factory.[9] A small firm might operate a single establishment. Larger firms, however, are often made up of two or more establishments. As corporations in this country have increased in size there has been a trend toward decentralization in decision-making. Broad policy is determined by the officers of the firm. But day-to-day management decisions are made at the level of the establishment. The establishment is also the basic unit for analytical purposes since data reported in the Census of Manufactures are based upon the establishment rather than the firm or the plant. Establishments are classified on the basis of their primary or principal products.

The classification of industries and sectors in an input-output table raises a number of technical problems which cannot be discussed here.[10] The aggregation problem – or the "index number problem" as it has been known in the past – is as old as the

---

[7] All of these operations may be carried on by a single firm in one or more plants. If this is the case we say it is an *integrated* firm, and we refer to this form of integration as vertical integration to distinguish it from the horizontal integration characteristic of many multiplant firms, such as chain stores, which specialize in one phase of economic activity.

[8] The 20 major industry groups are referred to as the *two-digit* classification. There is a further breakdown into *three-digit* and *four-digit* classifications. An example of the two-digit classification is number 22, Textile Mill Products. Under this, one three-digit classification is number 225, Knitting Mills. As part of the latter we find Full-fashioned Hosiery Mills (number 2251).

[9] In some cases an establishment may consist of more than one plant if these are engaged in the same kind of activity and are located within the same state.

[10] See for example Mathilda Holzman, "Problems of Classification and Aggregation," in Wassily Leontief, *et al.*, *Studies in the Structure of the American*

science of economic statistics. For present purposes we will assume that the industries in our hypothetical economy are classified on the basis of their principal products, and that within any industry the products are relatively homogeneous.

Direct Purchases and Technical Coefficients

After an input-output table has been constructed for a given year, a table of input or *technical coefficients* can be developed from it. By a technical coefficient we mean *the amount of inputs required from each industry to produce one dollar's worth of the output of a given industry.* Technical coefficients are calculated *for processing sector industries only,* and may be expressed either in monetary or physical terms. Our hypothetical table is expressed in cents per dollar of direct purchases.

Two steps are involved in the calculation of technical coefficients: Gross output is adjusted by subtracting inventory depletion during the period covered by the table to obtain *adjusted* gross output. Since gross outlays in the processing sector are identical with gross outputs in this sector, adjusted gross outputs in our hypothetical economy can be computed by subtracting the entries in row 7 from the entries of row 12 of Table 2–1. The results can then be entered as a new row at the bottom of the table. The second step in the calculation of technical coefficients consists of dividing all the entries in each industry's column by the *adjusted* gross output for that industry.

For example, the adjusted gross output for industry A is equal to 63 (total gross outlay minus gross inventory depletion). To compute the coefficients for column 1, each entry in this column is divided by 63, which gives the entries in column 1 of Table 2–2. Similarly, the adjusted gross output for industry B is 57, and this divided into each entry in column 2 of Table 2–1 gives column 2 of Table 2–2, and so on throughout the remainder of the table.

A specific illustration may make the meaning of Table 2–2 somewhat clearer. From it we see that each dollar's worth of pro-

Economy (New York: Oxford University Press, 1953), pp. 326–59, and Richard Stone, *Input-Output and National Accounts,* OEEC (1961), pp. 101–12.

duction in industry A will require direct purchases from other industries as follows:

Intraindustry transactions of 16c
Purchases by industry A from industry B of 8c
Purchases by industry A from industry C of.............. 11c
Purchases by industry A from industry D of.............. 17c
Purchases by industry A from industry E of 6c
Purchases by industry A from industry F of 3c
　　　　　Total *direct* purchases　　　　61c

TABLE 2–2

Input Coefficient Table*

Direct Purchases per Dollar of Output

Industries Purchasing

		A	B	C	D	E	F
Industries Producing	A	16c	26c	3c	5c	13c	13c
	B	8c	7c	18c	3c	8c	18c
	C	11c	4c	21c	3c	13c	7c
	D	17c	2c	5c	21c	16c	9c
	E	6c	0	3c	36c	8c	4c
	F	3c	11c	18c	15c	5c	13c

* This table has been reproduced on a tear-out sheet at the back of the book.

If the technical coefficients remain constant from year to year, or if they can be adjusted on the basis of new information, we can calculate the amount of direct purchases required from each industry along the left-hand side of Table 2–2, as a result of an increase (or decrease) in the output of one or more of the industries listed at the top of the table. If, for example, the output of industry B were increased by $100 (assuming constant technical coefficients), the direct inputs of industry B (purchases from other industries) would be increased by the following amounts:

Inputs from industry	would be increased by
A	$26
B (intraindustry)	7
C	4
D	2
E	—
F	11

The total increase in the value of *direct* inputs due to an increase of $100 in the output of industry B amounts to $50.

If the input coefficients are relatively stable or if they can be adjusted on the basis of new information, the usefulness of the table of direct coefficients is apparent. By making use of such a table, the management of a typical firm in industry B could tell in advance how much it would have to buy directly from each of its supplying industries when it adds to its own total production.

Stability Conditions for the Table of Technical Coefficients

The table of direct coefficients by itself is of limited usefulness because it shows only the "first-round" effects of a change in the output of one industry on the industries from which it purchases inputs. This table forms the basis, however, for a *general solution* of an input-output problem which will be discussed in the next section. Because of this it is important that the table of direct coefficients meet certain stability conditions. These are that: (a) *at least one column in the table add up to less than unity,* and (b) that *no column in the table add to more than unity.* The mathematical proof of these conditions is quite complex, and no attempt will be made to demonstrate these propositions here.[11] When the table is expressed in monetary terms, as is Table 2–2, it is intuitively clear that an industry cannot pay more for its inputs than it receives from the sale of its output. Also, the steps described

[11] For a proof in the case where all technical coefficients are positive see Robert Solow, "On the Structure of Linear Models," *Econometrica,* XX (January 1952), 29–46. See also Carl F. Christ, "A Review of Input-Output Analysis" in *Input-Output Analysis: An Appraisal* (Princeton: Princeton University Press, 1955), pp. 148–49.

above for computing input coefficients in the open, static model show that these conditions will be met if in each column the sum of entries in the payments rows (less the inventory row) is greater than inventory depletion. In practice, these entries are relatively large and the stability conditions are safely met.

Direct and Indirect Purchases

Table 2–2 shows the *direct* purchases that will be made by a given industry from all other industries within the processing sector for each dollar's worth of current output. But this does not represent the *total* addition to output resulting from additional sales to the final demand sector. An increase in final demand for the products of an industry within the processing sector (coming from households, for example) will lead to both direct and *indirect* increases in the output of all industries in the processing sector. If, for example, there is an increase in final demand for the products of industry A, there will be direct increases in purchases from industries B, C, and so on. But in addition, when industry B sells more of its output to industry A, B's demand for the products of industries C, D, etc., will likewise increase. And these effects will spread throughout the processing sector.

An integral part of input-output analysis is the construction of a table which shows the direct and indirect effects of changes in final demand. It shows the *total* expansion of output in all industries as a result of the delivery of one dollar's worth of output outside the processing sector by each industry. A "delivery outside the processing sector" means a sale to households, investors, foreign buyers, a government agency, or any other buyer included in the final demand sector.

There are various methods for computing the combined direct and indirect effects. One is an iterative or step-by-step method which will be illustrated. No attempt will be made, however, to go through all the calculations required to construct a table by this method even for our simple hypothetical example.

Let us assume a one-dollar increase in the demand for the products of industry A. This will increase intraindustry transactions by 16c (see row 1, column 1, of Table 2–2). Thus the gross output of industry A will increase *at least* $1.16. But when the output of industry A increases, the firms in this industry will step up their purchases from industry B. Sales from industry B to industry A will go up an additional 9c ($1.16 × .08) as a result of the increased activity in industry A. Similarly, sales from industry C to industry A will increase 13c ($1.16 × .11), and so on down column 1 of Table 2–2.

But the indirect effects do not stop here. When industry B expands its production because of an increase in final demand for the products of industry A, the increased demand thus generated will be felt by all other industries in the processing sector which sell to industry B. We could repeat the calculations made above to include each industry in the processing sector, then by adding up all the figures a table would gradually be built up which would show the total requirements, direct and indirect, resulting from the delivery of one dollar's worth of the products of each industry in the processing sector to the final demand sector.

Fortunately for the development of input-output economics there is an alternative method which can be used with high-speed electronic computing equipment to arrive at the same results. In technical terms this method involves taking the difference between an identity matrix and the input coefficient matrix (Table 2–2), and from this computing a transposed inverse matrix.[12] This table, on page 26, shows the *total* requirements, direct and indirect, *per dollar of delivery outside the processing sector.*

Table 2–3 contains some "rounding error." In computing the inverse, and in other computations to be discussed later, all figures were carried to six decimal places. To simplify the exposition, however, all numbers have been rounded off to the nearest cent.

What does Table 2–3 show? In Table 2–2, we saw that each dollar's worth of production in industry A required 16c of *intra*-industry transactions. But it will be recalled that these were *direct* purchases only. Table 2–3 shows that *total* intraindustry transactions will rise an additional 22c — to a total of 38c — for each dollar's worth of industry A's products delivered to the final demand sector. This is because when industry A's output rises it

---

[12] The meaning of these terms and an illustrative computation are given in Chapter 7.

TABLE 2–3
Direct and Indirect Requirements
per Dollar of Final Demand*

	A	B	C	D	E	F
A	$1.38	.25	.28	.41	.27	.23
B	.45	1.21	.16	.19	.12	.24
C	.27	.38	1.38	.23	.17	.39
D	.35	.25	.25	1.53	.65	.41
E	.35	.26	.31	.39	1.28	.25
F	.38	.35	.22	.30	.21	1.32

*This table has been reproduced on a tear-out sheet at the back of the book.

must buy more from B, C, and the others in the table. When B sells more to A it must buy more from A, C, etc. The same holds true for all the industries in our hypothetical economy. Thus Table 2–3 shows the total dollar production directly and indirectly required *from the industry at the top* for each dollar of delivery to final demand *by the industry at the left.* Each time A sells an additional dollar's worth of goods to households, government, or some other component of final demand, B's output goes up 25c, C's output increases 28c, and so on *across the first row* of Table 2–3. All other rows in this table are read in the same way.

In one respect the hypothetical example is not very realistic. Most of the transactions in Table 2–3 are quite large relative to an increase of *one dollar* in sales to final demand by the industry at the left-hand side of the table. This is because small numbers, and few zeros, were used in the hypothetical transactions table. As a result, the ratio of interindustry transactions to final demand is quite high. An actual input-output model will have smaller values in its counterpart of Table 2–3, and there will be much greater variation throughout the table than there is in our hypothetical example.

An actual table of direct and indirect requirements shows, for example, that the output of the agricultural sector depends upon the demand for processed foods, tobacco, textiles, leather products, and chemicals. Thus there will be fairly large entries in the cells where the agriculture *column* intersects the rows of these sectors. Most apparel products are sold directly to consumers, however, and the entries in the apparel *column* will be small.[13] In brief, some industries in the processing sector will show relatively large interindustry transactions. Such industries exhibit strong interdependence. Other industries use relatively few raw materials or intermediate products, but they may have substantial labor inputs. If households are not included in the processing sector—customarily they are not—such an industry will exhibit weak interdependence.

Stability Conditions for the Table of Direct and Indirect Coefficients

In an earlier section the stability conditions for the table of direct coefficients were given, and it was noted that in practice these conditions will generally be met. There is a fundamental condition that must also be met by the table of direct and indirect requirements (Table 2–3) known as the "Hawkins-Simon condition."[14] The mathematical proof of this condition given by Hawkins and Simon is much too complex to be discussed here, but its meaning can be made intuitively clear. Basically, the Hawkins-Simon condition states that *there can be no negative entries in the table of direct and indirect requirements*.[15] What would a negative entry in Table 2–3 mean? In essence it would mean that each time the industry with a negative entry expanded its sales to final demand, its direct and indirect input requirements would decline. Carried to the extreme this would mean that the more this industry expanded its output the less it would have to buy from other industries. This is clearly a logical contradiction and an economic absurdity.

---

[13] See Evans and Hoffenberg, *op. cit.,* p. 140.

[14] David Hawkins and H. A. Simon, "Some Conditions of Macroeconomic Stability," *Econometrica,* 17 (July–October 1949), 245–48.

[15] See William J. Baumol, *Economic Theory and Operations Analysis* (Englewood Cliffs, N. J.: Prentice-Hall, Inc., 1961), pp. 306–8.

The Hawkins-Simon condition is an important one. The appearance of one or more negative entries in a table of direct and indirect requirements per dollar of sales to final demand is a signal that something has gone wrong. There could have been a mistake in the construction of the transactions table, or computing errors in deriving the table of direct input coefficients. It is necessary then to go back, locate the cause of an obvious economic contradiction, and make the necessary adjustments or corrections.

Conclusions

Each *row* of Table 2–3 shows the *output* directly and indirectly required *from each sector* at the *top* of the table to support the delivery of $1.00 to final demand by the sector at the left of each row. Each *column* shows the output required for a *single* sector (directly and indirectly) to support $1.00 of delivery to final demand by *each* of the processing sectors.

Table 2–3 is a *general solution* of the hypothetical input-output system. It illustrates the principle of *economic interdependence*. The table can be used to show how a change in demand for the output of one sector stimulates production in other sectors. It shows the end result after all of the "feedback effects" have worked themselves out. The model illustrated here is a static one. No effort has been made to introduce the time lags that would be involved in achieving the equilibrium results given in Table 2–3. The dynamics of input-output analysis will be discussed briefly in Chapters 5 and 7.

Once a general solution or table of direct and indirect coefficients has been obtained, the input-output model can be used for a variety of analytical purposes. Some of the major uses will be discussed in the following chapter.

REFERENCES

CHENERY, HOLLIS B. and PAUL G. CLARK, *Interindustry Economics* (New York: John Wiley & Sons, Inc., 1959), pp. 13–65.

EVANS, W. DUANE and MARVIN HOFFENBERG, "The Interindustry Relations Study for 1947," *The Review of Economics and Statistics,* XXXIV (May 1952), 97–142.

LEONTIEF, WASSILY, *et al., Studies in the Structure of the American Economy* (New York: Oxford University Press, 1953).

National Bureau of Economic Research, *Input-Output Analysis: An Appraisal* (Princeton: Princeton University Press, 1955).

STONE, RICHARD, *Input-Output and National Accounts* (Paris: Organization for European Economic Co-Operation, June 1961), pp. 21–31.

3 Applications of Input-Output Analysis

Structural Analysis

The transactions table (Table 2–1) simultaneously describes the demand and supply relationships of an economy in equilibrium. It describes the economy as it is, not as it ought to be on the basis of some criterion or set of criteria. The table does not tell us whether the economy is operating at peak efficiency (e.g. full employment) or at less than peak efficiency. But it does show the final demand for goods and services and the interindustry transactions required to satisfy that demand.

If the input-output model did nothing more than describe the structural interdependence of the economy, it would be useful to analysts and policy-makers. It can do much more than that, however. If input-output tables are available for two or more countries, for example, they can be used for making a detailed *comparative* analysis of the economies involved. Such an analysis would reveal much more, for example, than a simple comparison of "stages of growth." It could be used by policy-makers in underdeveloped countries to help determine the types of investment which would do most to stimulate growth. As a matter of fact, input-output analysis has become an important development tool, and this particular application will be discussed further in Chapter 5.

Interindustry analysis can also be used to help solve problems in advanced industrial economies. Assume, for example, that an economy is operating at less than full employment because of a deficiency in aggregate demand.[1] It is not a difficult task to de-

[1] Inadequate aggregate demand is not the only cause of unemployment in an advanced economy. Structural changes in the economy, coupled with various kinds of labor immobility (industrial, occupational, and geographic), can also lead to unemployment. The issue of inadequate aggregate demand versus structural

termine the level of aggregate demand which would be required to achieve full employment. The necessary changes in the final demand sectors of the input-output table could be made, and by using the table of direct and indirect coefficients (Table 2–3), one could determine the levels of activity that would be required in all industries and sectors to achieve the goal of full employment. This use of input-output goes beyond description; it involves manipulation of the transactions table. The way in which this is done will be discussed in some detail in the following section.

As suggested in the preceding paragraph, an up-to-date input-output table can be used by policy-makers to project full-employment levels of over-all demand. But the usefulness of this technique is not limited to public policy-makers. Private businesses can make effective use of this analytical tool, particularly in connection with marketing programs.[2] Each row of an input-output table is in effect the marketing profile of an industry or sector. And the columns represent input patterns which tend to be more stable in the short run than the annual sales of many products. By projecting final sales, market analysts could forecast interindustry requirements for many products. They could thus build up more accurate *total* sales forecasts for the products of many industries than would be possible in the absence of data on interindustry transactions.

Input-Output as a Forecasting Tool

In this section we will be concerned with the technique of forecasting by means of input-output analysis. Some of the problems involved will be mentioned in passing, but these will be discussed in greater detail in a later section. Since a variety of analytic techniques are used in making economic forecasts, even a summary discussion would go beyond the scope of this book. It might be useful, however, to distinguish among three broad approaches to forecasting.

---

change as causes of unemployment has been widely debated in the United States in recent years, but this debate is not relevant to the present discussion. To illustrate a point, we are *assuming* that unemployment is due to inadequate demand.

[2] See W. Duane Evans, "Marketing Uses of Input-Output Data," *Journal of Marketing,* XVII (July 1952), 11–21.

Partial forecasting. Most forecasting involves the projection of one or more time series. The simplest method of partial forecasting is to fit a mathematical curve to an individual time series, and extrapolate this to some future date. This is a rudimentary forecasting technique which works well only in the case of a few "well-behaved" time series such as those which are closely correlated with population growth and rising income. One of the problems of partial forecasting, however, is that some time series are quite volatile; there are wide short-term variations around a trend line fitted to such series. The trend might be useful for long-range planning purposes, but wide variations around the trend line can result in misleading short-term forecasts. Another major problem of partial forecasting is that individual forecasts based upon time series might not add up to a meaningful total. In brief, there is always a problem of possible inconsistencies when individual time series are projected, regardless of the analytical technique used in making such projections.

The use of simultaneous equations. One way to avoid the problem of possible inconsistency among the projections of individual time series is to develop a model for the simultaneous projection of a group of time series. Models of this type consist of systems of equations, many of which contain a "stochastic" variable or error term. Such models avoid the problem of inconsistency. But if they include a limited number of time series this is still partial forecasting, and the results might be affected by an "outside" or exogenous disturbance. To avoid this problem some forecasters use a few highly aggregated time series which collectively describe the level of economic activity in the entire economy. Such models might result in fairly accurate forecasts. But the high degree of aggregation limits their usefulness. They can be helpful to policy-makers concerned with broad issues. But they are not of much use to businessmen and others concerned with anticipated levels of activity in specific industries or sectors.

Consistent forecasting. This term has been applied to the projection of a transactions table. When an input-output table is projected, "the output of each industry is consistent with the demands, both final and from other industries, for its products."[3]

---

[3] Clopper Almon, Jr., "Progress Toward a Consistent Forecast of the American Economy in 1970," a paper presented at the Conference on National Economic Planning, University of Pittsburgh, March 24–25, 1964 (mimeographed); p. 2.

There is no guarantee, of course, that a consistent forecast will turn out to be right. What the consistent forecast does is to insure that projections for individual industries and sectors will add up to a total projection (of Gross National Product, for example) if the structural relations of the economy do not change significantly over the projection period, or if allowance can be made for anticipated changes in the structural relations. By introducing additional variables, it is also possible to insure that investment and employment in each industry or sector will be consistent with its projected output, and that consumer demand and government expenditures will be consistent with projected disposable income.

One of the major problems involved in consistent forecasting is that of allowing for changes in the structural coefficients (Table 2–2) when long-term projections are being made. For short-term forecasts—for periods of two or three years—it is fairly safe to assume that the input coefficients will not change, or that they will not change significantly. In making long-term projections, for a ten-year period, for example, one cannot assume that input coefficients will remain constant. For such projections, it is necessary to use a dynamic input-output model, and more will be said about this in a later section.

There are two major steps involved in consistent forecasting: (1) It is necessary to make projections of each entry in the final demand sectors of the input-output table; then (2) a new transactions table is projected on the basis of the assumed changes in final demand. After the individual components of final demand have been projected, the individual final demand columns (columns 7 through 11 of Table 2–1) are added together to form a single column. This is referred to as the final demand column, or in technical language as the final demand *vector*.[4] When the final demand sectors have been combined into a single column, the transactions table is compressed as shown in Table 3–1.

The processing sector of Table 2–1 has been carried over intact to Table 3–1. But the five final demand columns have now been compressed into the single column shown in the table below.

In making an actual forecast, each of the final demand components (columns 7 through 11 of Table 2–1) would be projected independently. Only after this had been done would the individual

[4]The meaning of a vector is explained in Chapter 7.

TABLE 3-1

Transactions Table with Final Demand Column

		Industry Purchasing						Final Demand	Total Gross Output
		A	B	C	D	E	F		
Industry Producing	A	10	15	1	2	5	6	25	64
	B	5	4	7	1	3	8	31	59
	C	7	2	8	1	5	3	14	40
	D	11	1	2	8	6	4	7	39
	E	4	0	1	14	3	2	16	40
	F	2	6	7	6	2	6	17	46

columns be added to form a projected final demand vector. The table below shows the final demand column from Table 3-1 and a projected final demand for some future time period.

Assumed Changes in Final Demand

Industry	Original Final Demand	Projected Final Demand	Per Cent Change
A	25	30	+ 20%
B	31	26	− 16
C	14	17	+ 21.5
D	7	10	+ 43
E	16	15	− 6.5
F	17	20	+ 17.5

Note that in the hypothetical projections of final demand, the output of most industries is expected to increase. But the end-use demand for products made by industries B and E is expected to decline. These assumptions have been made deliberately to show what will happen to the projected transactions table when some industries are expected to expand their output while production in others is expected to decline. This is a realistic assumption for a dynamic economy in which some types of economic activity may contract even when there is rapid growth in other sectors of the economy. To some extent this might be the result of substitution. In the contrived example which we are discussing, industry B might represent coal mining while industry C might represent the oil and gas industry. The substitution of oil and gas for coal, in this example, would be the cause of the projected decline in B and the projected growth in C.

Once the individual final demand projections have been made and summed into a column vector, we are in a position to project a new transactions table. Since the final demand sectors have been combined into a single column—and only total final demand is shown—the projected transactions table will be limited to the processing sectors. After the projections of interindustry transactions representing intermediate demand have been completed, it would be possible to disaggregate the *projected* final demand column and reconstruct a completely new version of Table 2–1 for the target year. This would involve no particular problems since each of the components of final demand would have been projected independently in the first instance.

Assume that we are making a five-year projection of Table 2–1 on the basis of the changes in final demand given above. We also assume that during the projection period the technical coefficients of Table 2–2 remain constant. The results are given in Table 3–2. The projected interindustry transactions are shown in the upper part of each cell. The original transactions table, with final demand now shown as a single column, has been added to Table 3–2 with all of the original entries given in parentheses.[5]

[5] The computational steps for projecting a transactions table are as follows:

1. Compute *adjusted* projected final demand by first multiplying the original projected final demand by the ratio of inventory depletions to final demand in the base year, then subtracting this amount from the original projected final demand.

2. Multiply each *row* of the table of direct and indirect coefficients (Table 2–3) by the adjusted final demand figure for that row. The result will be another table of the same size as Table 2–3.

3. Sum the *columns* of the matrix obtained in step 2 to obtain new *adjusted total gross outputs* for each industry. Transfer the *row* that is thus obtained to the bottom of the table of direct coefficients (Table 2–2).

TABLE 3-2

Projected Transactions Table with Changes in Final Demand*

		A	B	C	D	E	F	Projected Final Demand	Projected Total Gross Output
				Industry Purchasing					
Industry Producing	A	11.728 (10)	15.488 (15)	1.222 (1)	2.460 (2)	5.790 (5)	7.199 (6)	30 (25)	74 (64)
	B	5.864 (5)	4.130 (4)	8.557 (7)	1.230 (1)	3.474 (3)	9.599 (8)	26 (31)	59 (59)
	C	8.210 (7)	2.065 (2)	9.779 (8)	1.230 (1)	5.790 (5)	3.599 (3)	17 (14)	48 (40)
	D	12.901 (11)	1.033 (1)	2.445 (2)	9.839 (8)	6.948 (6)	4.799 (4)	10 (7)	48 (39)
	E	4.691 (4)	0 (0)	1.222 (1)	17.218 (14)	3.474 (3)	2.400 (2)	15 (16)	44 (40)
	F	2.346 (2)	6.195 (6)	8.557 (7)	7.379 (6)	2.316 (2)	7.199 (6)	20 (17)	54 (46)

*Original transactions table, final demand, and total gross outputs shown in parentheses.

Although final demand for the products of industries B and E declined, the values of their interindustry transactions increased. The increases are smaller than those for the industries which registered gains in final sales, but in all cases there has been at least a slight gain. In our hypothetical example, the gains in interindustry transactions for industry B exactly offset the drop in demand for its products by households, government, and other

4. Multiply each column entry in the table of direct coefficients by the adjusted total gross output at the bottom of the column. The result is the processing sector of the projected transactions table.

5. To obtain the total gross output figures shown in Table 3-2, add the appropriate inventory adjustment which was subtracted in step 1 to the *adjusted* total gross outputs found in step 3.

6. Insert the original projected final demand figures as a column to the right of the projected processing sector, and insert the total gross output figures obtained in step 5 as a column to the right of final demand. The result is the projected transactions table illustrated by Table 3-2.

components of final demand, so that the total gross output of this industry remained unchanged. In the case of industry E, increases in interindustry transactions *more than* offset the decline in final demand so that its total gross output went up from 40 billion dollars to 44 billion. As one might expect, there were larger relative gains in total gross output for those industries which experienced increases in *both* final demand and in interindustry transactions.

In making an actual forecast there is one additional step which could be taken, but which will not be illustrated in this hypothetical example. After the new processing sector entries and the new total gross output figures had been obtained, the projected final demand vector could be disaggregated into the original components from which it was built up, and the same could be done for the rows in the payments sector. This would result in a new table exactly like Table 2–1. Since the objective of the projection is to obtain the interindustry transactions that would be needed to sustain projected levels of final demand, however, these steps are rarely carried out.

The above description of consistent forecasting sounds deceptively simple. As a matter of fact, assuming that an up-to-date transactions table is available, *short-term* consistent forecasting is a relatively simple matter. The accuracy of the interindustry projections will depend, of course, upon the accuracy with which the final demand projections can be made. But even if there is a certain amount of error in the projections of final demand, as one must expect, the resulting projections of interindustry transactions will be useful to economists, business analysts, and policy-makers. If such a forecast of the national economy were available, businessmen could adjust their individual production and employment schedules to conform to the over-all projections.

The above example of an input-output forecast is limited to the case of relatively short-term projections because the model upon which it is based is static; it assumes no change in technical coefficients. The input patterns in Table 2–2 are expected to be stable during the projection period. Technical coefficients do not change rapidly, and the small changes that might occur over a relatively short period would not lead to serious errors in the projected transactions table. Over a longer time span, however, the technical coefficients will be affected by three kinds of changes. These changes, and the effects which they will have upon the technical coefficients, are as follows:

Changes in relative prices. If the relative prices of factors of production change during the period covered by the projection, it is possible that input patterns, and hence some of the technical coefficients, will be changed. This will happen, however, only if some inputs can be substituted for others. This can be illustrated by a simple example. Assume that an industry is a large consumer of steel, but that on technological grounds it could just as easily use aluminum. If steel prices rise significantly during the period covered by the forecast, while aluminum prices remain stable (or possibly decline), this industry will substitute aluminum for steel. It is not necessary for the industry to make a complete switch from steel to aluminum in order to affect the input coefficients. But if its purchases of steel decline substantially and there is a corresponding rise in aluminum purchases, it is clear that the input coefficients in this industry's column and the steel and aluminum rows will change.

This illustration assumes that the table is sufficiently dis-aggregated to have separate rows and columns for the aluminum and steel industries. In a more highly aggregated table, which might include steel and aluminum in the same industry group, there would probably still be a change in the input coefficient as a result of the substitution, but the effects would be smaller than those in a more disaggregated table in which the steel and aluminum industries are considered separately.

Another substitution that might affect input coefficients is that of capital for labor. Even if we assume no change in technology, it is possible that firms will substitute machinery for labor if labor costs rise rapidly while the cost of capital does not change significantly during the projection period. When more machinery and less labor is used, a number of input coefficients can be affected. The relative share of total payments to households may be expected to decline; and when more machinery is used the inputs of electric energy may be expected to rise. While it is easy to exaggerate the effects of such substitutions on input coefficients over short periods of time, they would have to be taken into account in making a long-term projection.

The appearance of new industries. A long-term consistent forecast might be thrown off to some extent by the appearance of one or more new industries during the projection period. The rapid growth of the computer "industry" during the 1950s can be used to illustrate this point. If an input-output projection of the U.S. economy to 1960 had been made in 1950, assuming no change in technical coefficients, it would have failed to pick up the effects of the rapid growth of this new form of economic activity. Such a forecast would also have failed to register the effects of the rapidly growing space "industry."

The input requirements of the computer industry might not differ too radically from those of its predecessor, the "business machines" industry. Hence, a more aggregated projection of final demand for business machines might still have resulted in a useful consistent forecast. The rapid growth of the missile industry during the 1950s, with a relative decline in some parts of the aircraft industry, would have been much harder to project in 1950, however. Thus, a ten-year input-output forecast of the U.S. economy made in 1950 would no doubt have overstated the growth of the aircraft industry and would have understated the expansion of the missile "industry." Needless to say, such unexpected developments affect *all* types of forecasting. This does not mean that forecasting should be abandoned because such developments cannot be foreseen. What it does mean is that when some new form of economic activity appears on the horizon, earlier forecasts should be adjusted to take into account the effects of impending changes. The input-output model is sufficiently flexible and adaptable to allow for the introduction of such changes.

The effects of technological change on technical coefficients. One of the earliest criticisms of the input-output technique was that it assumed "fixed" technical coefficients whereas over a sufficiently long period of time new technological developments are bound to affect input patterns. But the effects of technological change on input coefficients can be handled more easily within the general framework of input-output analysis than the other types of changes mentioned above. The criticism that input coefficients are not "fixed" is not a serious one. What it means, however, is that in making long-term forecasts one cannot rely upon a static input-output model. While dynamic input-output analysis is still in its early stages, significant progress is being made. Dynamic models are much more complex than the static model discussed in this book, and no effort has been made to go into dynamic input-output analysis in detail. An example of how the static model can be adapted to take into account the effects of technological change, and thus used for making long-term projections, will be discussed in Chapter 6. And research is now under way which, it is hoped, will lead to improved dynamic models.[6] Operational dynamic models will not only improve the accuracy of forecasts, but will permit projections to be made for longer time periods.

Meanwhile, static input-output models are being used to make short-term forecasts, and the effectiveness of this technique has been demonstrated. Perhaps the outstanding example is the use of consistent input-output forecasts as part of "indicative planning" in France. The French experience with indicative, or non-coercive, planning has attracted worldwide attention. In some ways, indicative planning is a misnomer. The French economy is not centrally planned; that is, the French government does not establish production targets which must be met by all enterprises. On the contrary, the French economy is one in which resources are allocated and incomes are distributed largely by the market mechanism as in the United States.

What does happen is that the French Planning Commission makes detailed projections of output for the French economy for a specified future period.[7] An input-output model plays an

---

[6] Wassily Leontief, "Dynamic Analysis," in Wassily Leontief, *et al., Studies in the Structure of the American Economy* (New York: Oxford University Press, 1953), pp. 53–90; Clopper Almon, "Consistent Forecasting in a Dynamic Multi-Sector Model," *The Review of Economics and Statistics,* XLV (May 1963), pp. 148–62; Almon, "Numerical Solution of a Modified Leontief Dynamic System for Consistent Forecasting or Indicative Planning," *Econometrica,* XXXI (October 1963), 665–78; Almon, "Progress Toward a Consistent Forecast of the American Economy in 1970," paper presented at the Conference on National Planning, University of Pittsburgh, March 24–25, 1964 (mimeographed); Anne P. Carter, "Incremental Flow Coefficients for a Dynamic Input-Output Model with Changing Technology," in Tibor Barna (ed.), *Structural Interdependence and Economic Development* (New York: St.Martin's Press, 1963), pp. 277–302; Per Sevaldson, "Changes in Input-Output Coefficients," *idem,* pp. 303–28.

[7] See *French and Other National Plans for Economic Growth,* European Committee for Economic and Social Progress (CEPES) (New York: Committee for Economic Development, 1963). For a discussion of the generally favorable attitude of French businessmen toward indicative planning see "Planning Debate Comes to the U.S.," *Business Week* (May 25, 1963), 140–44.

important part in this forecasting procedure. In essence, a detailed forecast of final demand is prepared, and from this projected levels of interindustry transactions are computed as in the example given earlier in this chapter. The final demand for automobiles is projected, for example, and from the input-output forecast, the French steel industry can determine how an increase in automobile production will affect its output. The coal industry, in turn, can then see how its production will be affected by the expansion of steel output. The effects of anticipated changes in final demand on each industry can be traced back, through the input-output table, to all other industries.

Consistent forecasting provides an important guide to public policy-makers. But such forecasts are also extremely useful to the management of an individual enterprise. The director of a firm will usually have a pretty good idea of his share of the total market the firm serves. He will also know whether his share of the market is growing, declining, or remaining relatively constant. Given an accurate forecast of the total sales his industry can anticipate in a particular year—intermediate sales as well as final sales—the manager of the firm will be in an excellent position to adjust to the market changes which have been projected.

Consistent forecasting as it has been practiced in France has been quite successful. The French businessman feels somewhat less uncertain about future market prospects than his counterpart in other countries where such information is not available. It is also possible that the forecasting procedure itself contributes to the realization of projected output levels. Since each enterprise in a market economy is dependent upon the levels of activity in other enterprises, the reduction of uncertainty can contribute to the realization of projected output levels. There is some evidence that this has been the case in France, and that part of the success of indicative planning in that country is a result of the availability of more accurate market forecasts than was true in the past.

It should be emphasized that there is no need for any kind of planning—noncoercive or otherwise—for consistent forecasting to be useful. The availability of an accurate consistent forecast would be just as helpful to businessmen in the United States as it has been to businessmen in France. Efforts to provide a consistent forecast of the United States economy will be discussed briefly in a later chapter.

Impact or Multiplier Analysis

Economists have long been interested in measuring the *total* impact upon employment, income, and output resulting from a given change in investment. One of the more useful analytical techniques developed by J. M. Keynes, based upon the earlier work of R. S. Kahn, was that of the multiplier. Since Keynes dealt in broad aggregates, his income and employment multipliers were also highly aggregated. Keynes pointed out that if a certain amount of income were injected into the economy, consumer spending would rise although by an amount less than the injection of income. The proportion of added income spent by consumers became someone else's "new" income. The latter, in turn, spent some fraction of their additional income, and this procedure continued through several "rounds" of spending. Keynes noted that if the marginal propensity to consume—that is, the difference between two successive levels of consumer spending associated with two successive levels of income—could be measured, the income multiplier could also be estimated. The approximate total addition to national income which would result from a given injection of "new" income would be the multiplier times this income increment.[8]

The concept of an aggregate multiplier is a useful one, and it plays an important role in public policy decisions. This concept was used, for example, in determining the size of the tax cut which followed enactment of the Revenue Act of 1964.

Aggregative multipliers are useful analytical tools, but they do not show the details of how multiplier effects are worked out throughout the economy. And at times economists and businessmen are more interested in the details than in the over-all impact. Assume, for example, that a decision has been made to stimulate economic activity by means of investment in public works. There will be an immediate impact on the construction industry, but how will the effects of stepped-up construction activity ramify throughout the economy? Or consider the case of changes in international trade: If import restrictions on certain products are relaxed, how will changes in the pattern of international trade

---

[8] For a discussion of the aggregate multiplier concept, see Dudley Dillard, *The Economics of John Maynard Keynes* (Englewood Cliffs, N. J.: Prentice-Hall, Inc., 1948), pp. 85–100.

affect specific industries? In a similar vein, what effects will a reduction in defense spending have upon the economy as a whole? The impacts on the industries most directly affected can be measured with little difficulty. But when one recognizes the interdependence of economic activities, it is apparent that the *total* impact will not be limited to those industries directly affected.

In this section, we will discuss sectoral multipliers which are derived from an input-output model. The first step in the development of sectoral multipliers is to "close" the basic transactions table with respect to households. This has been done in Table 3-3, which is the original transactions table (Table 2-1) with households (row and column H) moved into the processing sector. Table 3-3 also differs from Table 2-1 in that the payments and final demand sectors (now minus households) are shown as a single row and column. In other respects, the basic transactions table remains unchanged.

TABLE 3-3

Transactions Table with Households Included in Processing Sectors

		Sector Purchasing							Final Demand	Total Gross Output
		A	B	C	D	E	F	H		
Sector Producing	A	10	15	1	2	5	6	14	11	64
	B	5	4	7	1	3	8	17	14	59
	C	7	2	8	1	5	3	5	9	40
	D	11	1	2	8	6	4	4	3	39
	E	4	0	1	14	3	2	9	7	40
	F	2	6	7	6	2	6	8	9	46
	H	16	18	7	5	7	9	1	9	72
Payments Sector		9	13	7	2	9	8	14		
Total Gross Outlays		64	59	40	39	40	46	72		

In the original transactions table, it was not necessary for the sum of the household row to equal the sum of the household column. It will be recalled that the only restriction in that table was that the sum of *all* final demand columns had to equal the sum of *all* rows in the payments sector. When any row and its corresponding column are moved into the processing sector, however, the sum of the row entries must equal the sum of the column entries. Thus, in moving the household row and column into the processing sector, it was necessary to reconcile the row and column totals by adjusting some of the other entries in the final demand and payments sectors. In making this reconciliation in the hypothetical table the smaller (column) total was chosen.

After the transactions table has been closed with respect to households, a new table of technical coefficients must be computed. Table 3-4, which corresponds to Table 2-2, gives the input coefficients associated with the new transactions table. The coefficients in the first six rows and the first six columns are identical with those given in Table 2-2. Note, however, that the household coefficients are quite large in the first six columns and quite small in the seventh. This indicates that labor inputs are important in the processing sector, but that there are small inputs

TABLE 3-4

Input Coefficient Table Including Households in Processing Sector

Direct Purchases Per Dollar of Output[1]

	A	B	C	D	E	F	H
A	16c	26c	3c	5c	13c	13c	19c
B	8c	7c	18c	3c	8c	18c	24c
C	11c	4c	21c	3c	13c	7c	7c
D	17c	2c	5c	21c	16c	9c	6c
E	6c	0	3c	36c	8c	4c	12c
F	3c	11c	18c	15c	5c	13c	11c
H	25c	32c	18c	13c	18c	20c	1c

[1] Rounded to nearest cent.

from households to households where such transactions would largely be limited to domestic help.

When a transactions table is closed with respect to households, one of the important characteristics of the processing sector industries becomes apparent, namely their relative labor intensity. Our hypothetical table shows, for example, that industry B is quite labor-intensive. It utilizes 32 cents worth of labor inputs for every dollar of output. Industry D, however, uses much less labor — its labor input amounts to 13 cents per dollar of output. This would be a capital-intensive industry in the hypothetical model.

The next step in making an input-output multiplier analysis is to compute the *direct and indirect* requirements per dollar of final demand for the new system which includes households in the processing sector. The procedure for doing this is exactly the same as that briefly described in Chapter 2 (and discussed in mathematical terms in Chapter 7). The problem is the same — that of finding a general solution to the new transactions table by computing a transposed inverse matrix of the difference between Table 3–4 and an identity matrix. The results of this operation are given in Table 3–5. Each entry in this table shows the *total* dollar production directly and indirectly required from the industry at the top of the table per dollar of deliveries to final

TABLE 3-5
Direct and Indirect Requirements Per Dollar of Final Demand with Households Included with Processing Sector

	A	B	C	D	E	F	H
A	1.992669	.798831	.608516	.781989	.656877	.632756	1.232486
B	1.053592	1.745810	.483929	.555901	.497985	.635246	1.212641
C	.828823	.889082	1.680955	.578114	.519785	.765752	1.131703
D	.940778	.785017	.567515	1.894111	1.019691	.798795	1.195729
E	.905022	.750192	.600672	.723617	1.626740	.617691	1.105895
F	.955246	.870436	.531722	.648535	.572789	1.703084	1.158277
H	.978913	.875536	.522263	.599521	.613559	.645994	1.965217

Each entry shows total dollar production directly and indirectly required from industry at top per dollar of deliveries to final demand by industry at left.

demand by the industry at the left-hand side of the table. We use the term *industry* loosely here to include households.

There is one striking difference between Table 3–5 and its earlier counterpart, Table 2–3. In the original table, all of the numbers along the diagonal from the upper left to the lower right are greater than one. All other numbers in that table are less than one. In Table 3–5, we note again that all numbers along the diagonal are greater than one, but so are those in some of the other cells, including all of the entries in column H.

All tables of direct and indirect requirements per dollar of final demand have diagonal entries greater than one because in the general solution of the system of equations the output of each industry is increased by one dollar.[9] Typically, however, large entries off the diagonal, such as those in column H of Table 3–5, are found in the table of direct and indirect requirements only when households are moved into the processing sector.

The relatively large numbers in column H of Table 3–5 are not particularly realistic. Their size stems from the fact that the numbers which were arbitrarily inserted into the original transactions table gave a larger weight to household inputs than would ordinarily be the case in a model based upon actual data. Even in a model based on actual data, however, some of the entries in the household column of the table of direct and indirect requirements (when households are included in the processing sector) will be greater than one.[10]

From the data in Table 3–5, it is now possible to compute income multipliers for the industries included in the processing sector of the *original* transactions table (Table 2–1). Various types of multipliers can be computed, and two of these are illustrated by Table 3–6. The illustrative multipliers in this table have been computed by the methods used by Hirsch in his input-output study of the St. Louis metropolitan area. The multipliers and the details of their calculation are given in Table 3–6.

---

[9] This is accomplished by subtracting the table of direct coefficients from an *identity matrix*. The latter is a matrix which has ones in every diagonal cell and zeros everywhere else. For further discussion of this point see Chapter 7.

[10] See for example Werner Z. Hirsch, "Interindustry Relations of a Metropolitan Area," *The Review of Economics and Statistics*, XLI (November 1959), table opposite page 368.

TABLE 3-6

Hypothetical Income Interactions

Sector	Direct income change (1)	Direct and indirect income change (2)	Indirect income change (3)	Type I multiplier (4)	Direct, indirect and induced income change (5)	Induced income change (6)	Indirect and induced income change (7)	Type II multiplier (8)
A	.25	.63	.38	2.52	1.23	.60	.98	4.92
B	.32	.62	.30	1.94	1.21	.59	.89	3.78
C	.18	.58	.40	3.22	1.13	.55	.95	6.28
D	.13	.61	.48	4.69	1.20	.59	1.07	9.23
E	.18	.56	.38	3.11	1.11	.55	.93	6.17
F	.20	.59	.39	2.95	1.16	.57	.96	5.80

(1) Column 1 is the household *row* of Table 3–4.
(2) Column 2 is the sum of [(each *row* entry of Table 2–3) × (the household coefficient of the corresponding *column* of Table 3–4)] .
(3) Column 2 minus column 1.
(4) Column 2 divided by column 1.
(5) The household *column* of Table 3–5.
(6) Column 5 minus column 2.
(7) Column 3 plus column 6.
(8) Column 5 divided by column 1.

Source: Example based on methods used by Werner Z. Hirsch, "Interindustry Relations of a Metropolitan Area," *The Review of Economics and Statistics,* XLI (November 1959), 364–65.

The Type I multiplier is sometimes referred to as a "simple" income multiplier since it takes into account only the direct and indirect changes in income resulting from an increase of one dollar in the output of all the industries in the processing sectors. The Type II multiplier is a more realistic measure which takes into account the direct and indirect effects indicated by the input-output model *plus* the *induced* changes in income resulting from increased consumer spending.[11] Thus for each sector the Type II multiplier will always be larger than its Type I counterpart.

The details of the calculations of each column in Table 3–6 are given in the footnotes to the table and need not be repeated here. It should be noted, however, that to compute the direct and indirect *income* changes shown in column 2, both the *original* table of direct and indirect effects (Table 2–3) and the households coefficients taken from the table of technical coefficients with households in the processing sector (Table 3–4) are used. Each row entry in the original inverse table is multiplied by the corresponding household coefficient of Table 3–4. These products are then summed to get the entries in column 2 of Table 3–6. The remaining entries in this table (except column 5, which is taken directly from Table 3–5) are computed as indicated in the footnotes.

What do these multipliers show? First, they reveal that different amounts of income are generated by different sectors of the economy even if we assume that each sector expands its output by the same amount. The Type I multipliers are limited to the direct and indirect effects on income of a given change in output, but the Type II multipliers also show "the chain reaction of inter-industry reactions in income, output, and once more on consumer expenditures."[12]

The greater the degree of interdependence within the economy, or conversely the lesser its dependence on imports, the greater will be the direct income changes. Because of this, income multipliers for the United States will be larger than those for an individual state.[13] It does not follow, however, that large direct in-

---

[11] See F. T. Moore, "Regional Economic Reaction Paths," *American Economic Review*, XLV (May 1955), 139–40.

[12] Werner Z. Hirsch, *op. cit.*, p. 364.

[13] Moore, *op. cit.*, pp. 138–39.

come changes are associated with large multipliers. For example, industry B in our hypothetical model is quite labor-intensive, while industry D is capital-intensive. A labor-intensive industry will produce a larger direct income change than one which is capital-intensive (see the entries in column 1, Table 3–6). But by the time direct *and indirect* income changes are taken into account, these differences might be eliminated or reversed (see the entries for B and D in column 2 of Table 3–6). The labor-intensive industry in our example showed the larger direct income change, but the reverse is true when we examine *indirect* income changes. Thus even in the "simple" or Type I multiplier, the income effects of the capital-intensive industry are larger than those of the labor-intensive industry. The reasons for this are fairly clear. An industry which uses a great deal of labor but not many other inputs will probably have fewer interactions with other industries than one which utilizes a considerable amount of capital equipment. When an industry which uses a great deal of capital expands its output the "chain reaction" this sets off will spread throughout many sectors of the economy.

There are some technical problems involved in computing income multipliers which can only be mentioned briefly here. First, it should be noted that most empirical input-output multipliers have been local or regional, and among the problems involved in conducting regional input-output studies are those resulting from the lack of data on consumer spending patterns for small areas. In computing his Type II income multipliers, Hirsch assumed that changes in consumer spending were proportional to changes in income. And he fully recognized that because of this assumption he had overstated the income effects of changes in final demand. In a similar study, Moore and Petersen computed sectoral consumption functions.[14] Because they were unable to obtain data for the area they studied (Utah), national consumption figures were used to compute the sectoral consumption functions for the state.[15] In addition, because of data limitations,

[14] A consumption function is an equation which shows the proportion of an *increase* in income which is spent on consumption. A sectoral consumption function is one which shows how much of a given change in income will be spent in a particular sector.

[15] Frederick T. Moore and James W. Petersen, "Regional Analysis: An Interindustry Model of Utah," *The Review of Economics and Statistics,* XXXVII (November 1955), 376–77.

their consumption functions were much more aggregated than their basic input-output model.

This is not a criticism of the Hirsch and Moore-Petersen studies. The authors are fully aware of the limitations of their consumer data, and specifically point out the effects which their assumptions, or the use of national data, had on the regional multipliers they computed. Finally, one should not exaggerate the limitations of sectoral multipliers computed from regional input-output models because of the underlying assumptions about consumer behavior. For many analytical purposes they are more useful and revealing than aggregate multipliers which relate only to the economy as a whole.

Employment Multipliers

There are times when the analyst is interested in measuring the employment effects of a change in demand as well as the income effects. Once an input-output table has been constructed, it is possible to compute employment multipliers, although different methods are employed than the one described above for computing income multipliers. Two methods for computing employment multipliers will be described briefly in this section, although illustrative examples will not be given since the basic concepts are the same as those described in the previous section.

The Isard-Kuenne method. This is a method for computing employment multipliers used to project estimated total employment in the Greater New York–Philadelphia region as a result of the expansion of the steel industry in the area.[16] Computationally, this method is related to the iterative technique for obtaining estimates of the direct and indirect requirements per dollar of sales to final demand discussed briefly in Chapter 2, and described in detail by Chenery and Clark.[17]

[16] Walter Isard and Robert E. Kuenne, "The Impact of Steel Upon the Greater New York–Philadelphia Industrial Region," *The Review of Economics and Statistics,* XXXV (November 1953), 289–301. For another application of this technique, involving a different industry and region, see Ronald E. Miller, "The Impact of the Aluminum Industry on the Pacific Northwest: A Regional Input-Output Analysis," *The Review of Economics and Statistics,* XXXIX (May 1957), 200–9.

[17] Hollis B. Chenery and Paul G. Clark, *Interindustry Economics* (New York: John Wiley & Sons, Inc., 1959), pp. 28–29.

Isard and Kuenne base their approach on the "agglomeration effect" of the location of a new industry in an area. This is a term taken from location theory, and it refers to the clustering of various kinds of economic activities in the general vicinity of a newly located firm in a basic industry. It is economical for establishments in some industries to locate near the source of supply of their raw material if this raw material is heavy and bulky with relatively high transport costs. If the firm also expects to find a substantial market for its products close to its raw-material source, there will be an even stronger tendency toward agglomeration.[18] In the case of a new steel mill, various types of steel-fabricating establishments tend to be attracted to it. Examples include manufacturers of tinware, hand tools, agricultural machinery, metal-working machinery, business machines, and a wide variety of other products which contain substantial quantities of steel and in which there is a significant amount of "value added" by the manufacturing process.

The first step in the Isard-Kuenne analysis was to estimate the agglomeration effect by analyzing the clustering of establishments around a similar basic installation in other areas with some of the characteristics of the region under study. The next step was to estimate the shifts in production that would occur between older areas and the one in which the new facility was being located because of the shift in markets which was expected to occur. Following this, estimates of production-worker employment were made for each of the "satellite" industries which were expected to be attracted to the new basic industry. Up to this point, the analysis depended heavily upon location theory and informed judgment.

The next step was to estimate the "bill of goods" which would have to be furnished to the area. This consisted of all inputs which would be absorbed by the basic industry plus the inputs of the "satellite" industries which would be attracted to it by the agglomeration effect. This is the point at which input-output analysis was introduced into the study. To construct the bill of goods an input-output table with households in the processing sector (similar to Table 3–3) was required. Each of the coef-

---

[18]Obviously not all of the output of a firm using the heavy and bulky raw material can be sold in a local market, but the firm will still have a strong incentive to locate near its source of raw materials to economize on transport costs.

ficients in this table was multiplied by the dollar volume of its expected production derived from the employment estimates mentioned above. This was done for both the basic and the "satellite" activities to obtain the *total* initial input requirements. Following this, the minimum input requirements *to be produced in the area* were estimated. There is no precise formula for the estimation of local area input requirements. The figures were derived by Isard and Kuenne by again relying upon location theory and informed judgment.

After all the estimates had been made, a table was constructed listing the basic industry and all other industries (including the new "satellite" industries) in the area in a column. This was followed by a column showing the total input requirements, and a second column showing the *percentage* of input requirements which would be produced in the area. The employment multiplier was then derived by computing a series of "rounds of expansion." The first round was computed by applying the percentage of input requirements to be produced in the area to the total input requirements. This procedure was applied successively until several "rounds" had been computed. Even with the application of a constant percentage of input requirements from the local area, each of the new "rounds" tended to be significantly smaller than the one before.[19] After each of the "rounds" had been computed, they were added together to obtain the "sum of round expansions." From this the total addition to employment was derived on the basis of earlier relationships between employment and production.

Isard and Kuenne estimated that the new steel mill would employ about 11,700 workers. The agglomeration effect was expected to attract metal-fabricating establishments which would employ an additional 77,000 workers. Thus an estimated 88,700 new jobs were expected in the area as a *direct* result of the new steel mill. But on the basis of their employment multipliers, Isard and Kuenne estimated that an additional 70,000 new jobs would open up in the area due to the *indirect* effects of the expansion of the basic steel industry in the region. Thus the estimated *total*

---

[19] Only six "rounds" (plus some extrapolation) were required to estimate the *total* expansion of input requirements due to the location of the new steel mill in this area.

employment impact on the area amounted to about 158,700 new jobs.[20]

The Isard-Kuenne method can be used if an up-to-date input-output table is available so that the input requirements for the basic and "satellite" industry can be obtained. When this method is applied to a region, it further assumes that the coefficients of a national table apply to the area being analyzed. More will be said about this assumption in the next section.

The Moore-Petersen method of computing employment multipliers. The Isard-Kuenne method was devised to measure the *total* employment impact on a region resulting from the location of a new basic industry in that area. It makes use of national coefficients to estimate the inputs of both the basic industry and the satellite industries expected to cluster around the former. There is no alternative to this approach since the Isard-Kuenne method was designed to *project* the total employment inpact of a new basic industry on an area. Even if close estimates of total employment in the basic industry had been available at the time of the analysis, there would have been no data on the "satellite" industries since such industries move into an area only *after* the basic industry is in operation. Thus the Isard-Kuenne method is limited in its application to the specialized situation discussed in the preceding section.

The Moore-Petersen method can only be used if a regional model, with regional coefficients, is available.[21] It is, however, a more general model designed to provide estimates of total regional employment effects, industry by industry, due to a change in final demand for the output of one or more industries in the region.

The Moore-Petersen employment multipliers are based upon *employment-production functions* which are computed for each industry in the table. The employment-production function measures the relationship between total employment (in man-years) in each industry and the gross output of that industry expressed in millions of dollars. In their Utah study, all of the production functions computed by Moore and Petersen were

---

[20] For the detailed results of the multiplier estimates see Isard and Kuenne, *op. cit.,* p. 297.

[21] For a complete discussion see Moore and Petersen, *op. cit.,* pp. 377–79.

linear; that is, they are simple equations which state that changes in employment are proportional to changes in output. The *slopes* of the employment-production functions are different, however, which tells us that employment in some industries will rise more than in others if we assume identical changes in the gross outputs of all industries. The slope of each employment-production function, which measures the rate of change of employment as output changes, is used to measure the *direct* change in employment associated with a one-million-dollar change in final demand.

To obtain the direct plus indirect effects, each of the direct and indirect coefficients (see Table 2–3) is multiplied by the appropriate employment function (the number representing the *slope* of each employment-production function), and the results are added across each row of the table. This gives the direct and indirect employment effects of a change in final demand of one million dollars in each industry. A set of "simple" interindustry employment multipliers for the region—analogous to the Type I income multipliers—are then obtained by dividing the direct plus indirect effects by the direct effects only.

To measure the direct, indirect, and *induced* employment changes—similar to the Type II income multipliers—Moore and Petersen used both their employment-production functions and the set of *consumption functions* mentioned earlier. Like the employment-production functions, their consumption functions are linear; they state that changes in consumption are proportional to changes in income.[22]

The logic behind the linking of consumption changes and employment changes is as follows. An initial change in final demand will lead to direct plus indirect changes in output, and these lead to the employment changes described by the "simple" employment multiplier. The change in employment, in turn, leads to a change in income, and hence to a change in consumer demand. Each of these changes sets off a "chain reaction" which leads to further adjustment in output, employment, income, and consumer demand, with each "round" of new effects being smaller than the one before. In a manner similar to that used by Isard and Kuenne, it is then possible to estimate the *total* employment

[22]Only one of the consumption functions is both linear and *homogeneous;* that is, when this consumption function (for utilities, trade, and service) is plotted on a graph, the straight line goes through the zero origin.

change by computing a number of successive "rounds" of changes in output, income, consumer spending, and employment. The results are estimates of the direct, indirect, and induced employment changes resulting from a given change (up or down) in output for each industry included in the table. The final step is to compute the *total* employment multiplier by dividing the direct, indirect, and induced employment changes by the direct employment changes only. Because the induced effects have been added to direct and indirect effects, the total multiplier for each industry will always be larger than the "simple" multiplier described briefly above.

Feasibility Tests and Sensitivity Analysis

The advantages of consistent forecasts to the business community were discussed earlier in this chapter, where it was also noted that such forecasts can be useful to public policy-makers. For example, consistent forecasts are basic to sensitivity analysis, and they can be used in making feasibility tests. The objective of a sensitivity analysis is to determine those elements or components of the economy which are more sensitive than others to alternative patterns of growth. This is one of the reasons that a series of economic growth studies is now being conducted by the U. S. Department of Labor, in cooperation with other government agencies and private research organizations.[23] The Department of Labor is making a series of five- and ten-year consistent projections, based upon alternative assumptions about rates and patterns of economic growth, to assist the federal government in developing and implementing various national economic policies.

The specific objectives of this program are the construction of an economic framework for: (1) developing estimates of employment in considerable occupational and industrial detail, and (2) providing the basis for evaluating the effects of various long-range government programs on the rest of the economy. Among these are public works, farm programs, defense expenditures, the

[23] Although the bulk of the work on this project is being conducted by the Department of Labor, an interagency planning and coordinating committee has been established to guide the program. The economic growth studies will be discussed further in Chapter 6.

space program, urban renewal, and the economic effects of disarmament.

The long-term economic growth studies are based upon various assumptions about levels of employment and unemployment. Since one policy objective of the federal government is that of maintaining full employment, one set of projections will assume that this goal has been reached. It will then be possible to determine the levels of economic activity which will be required in the various industries and sectors of the economy to maintain this state.

The sensitivity studies will include analysis of the effects of change in foreign trade patterns on domestic employment and production, and the expansion of various types of public works programs. Closely allied to sensitivity studies are various kinds of feasibility tests. A question might be raised, for example, about the feasibility of achieving a certain level of employment by a given target date. What will this involve in terms of final demand and interindustry relationships? What bottlenecks, if any, are likely to be encountered as an economy moves from a position of relatively high-level unemployment to full employment? In analyzing these and other problems, still other questions might be raised: Will the resources be available domestically to achieve the "product-mix" of a projected level of final demand? If not, what implications will this have for international trade?

One of the characteristics of a dynamic economy is that its basic structure changes over time. In the American economy, for example, the long-term trend of employment in agriculture has been steadily downward. Because of rapid advances in productivity, employment in the goods-producing sectors of the economy has increased only slowly. The major gains in employment have been in the trades and services, and in government — particularly state and local government. In making a useful long-term consistent forecast of an economy, it is necessary to take such major shifts into account. It is also necessary to consider projected increases in productivity and, if possible, the effects of relative changes in prices. The long-term projections being made by the Department of Labor and other cooperating governmental agencies and private research organizations will be based upon the interrelationships of demand, production, resources, income, and prices. The task is a formidable one. Even if there are errors in the projections (and there undoubtedly will be), the results should prove useful. They will provide guidelines to policy-makers—as well as to businessmen—who must prepare to meet the changes in the economy anticipated during the coming decade.

REFERENCES

ALMON, CLOPPER, JR., "Consistent Forecasting in a Dynamic Multi-Sector Model," *The Review of Economics and Statistics*, XLV (May 1963), 148–62.

_____, "Numerical Solution of a Modified Leontief Dynamic System for Consistent Forecasting or Indicative Planning," *Econometrica*, XXXI (October 1963), 665–78.

_____, "Progress Toward a Consistent Forecast of the American Economy in 1970," paper presented at the Conference on National Economic Planning, University of Pittsburgh, March 24–25, 1964 (mimeographed).

European Committee for Economic and Social Progress, *French and Other National Economic Plans for Growth* (New York: Committee for Economic Development, June 1963).

HIRSCH, WERNER Z., "Interindustry Relations of a Metropolitan Area," *The Review of Economics and Statistics*, XLI (November 1959), 360–69.

ISARD, WALTER and ROBERT E. KUENNE, "The Impact of Steel Upon the Greater New York–Philadelphia Industrial Region," *The Review of Economics and Statistics*, XXXV (November 1953), 289–301.

LEONTIEF, WASSILY, "Dynamic Analysis," *Studies in the Structure of the American Economy* (New York: Oxford University Press, 1953), pp. 53–90.

_____ and MARVIN HOFFENBERG, "The Economic Effects of Disarmament," *Scientific American*, CCIV (April 1961), 3–11.

MOORE, FREDERICK T., "Regional Economic Reaction Paths," *American Economic Review*, XLV (May 1955), 133–55.

_____ and JAMES W. PETERSEN, "Regional Analysis: An Interindustry Model of Utah," *The Review of Economics and Statistics*, XXXVII (November 1955), 368–83.

U. S. Department of Labor, *Research Program of Economic Growth Studies*, August 22, 1962 (mimeographed), pp. 1–19.

4 Regional and Interregional Input-Output Analysis

The initial development of input-output theory, and the early empirical work in interindustry analysis, was national in scope.[1] Since the end of World War II, however, there has been a great deal of interest in regional economic analysis. And as Charles Tiebout has said: "It is not too much of an overstatement to say that post-World War II regional research has been almost completely dominated by regional applications of input-output models. Whatever the form of the variations, the basic input-output theme is present."[2] This interest in regional input-output analysis is not surprising. There has been a strong emphasis on quantitative research in economics since the end of World War II, and the input-output model lends itself readily to regional and interregional applications. In this chapter, we can only touch upon the major developments, and refer primarily to those studies which have contributed something new to the development of regional and interregional input-output theory or to the empirical implementation of input-output models. Some of the applications of input-output analysis discussed in the preceding chapter — notably the development of income and employment multipliers — have regional as well as national applications. In fact, most of the work on sectoral income and employment multipliers has been at the regional rather than at the national level. Some other

[1] See Wassily Leontief, *The Structure of American Economy,* 1919–1939 (New York: Oxford University Press, 1951).

[2] Charles M. Tiebout, "Regional and Interregional Input-Output Models: An Appraisal," *The Southern Economic Journal,* XXIV (October 1957), 140. For a listing of regional and interregional studies in the United States and other countries, see Charlotte E. Taskier, *Input-Output Bibliography 1955–1960* (New York: United Nations, 1961), pp. 52–66, and *Input-Output Bibliography 1960–1963* (New York: United Nations, 1964), pp. 27–40.

applications will be developed in the following sections, and some of the problems unique to regional input-output analysis will be discussed briefly.

Interregional and Multiregional Input-Output Analysis

There are a number of variations of input-output analysis at the regional level, and input-output studies with a regional orientation can be classified in a number of ways. One major distinction is between interregional (or multiregional) models and regional models. In the former, a single model includes more than one region, while regional models are similar to national models except that they cover a smaller geographic area. In this section we will be concerned only with models of the interregional or multiregional variety.

A further distinction can be made between *balanced* regional models and what have been called *pure* interregional models. A balanced regional model is constructed by disaggregating a national input-output table into its component regions. The pure interregional model is implemented by aggregating a number of regional tables, and the latter may or may not include all the regions in the national economy.[3] As Isard has pointed out, however, "the two models should not be viewed as alternatives. Rather they are complements. The Leontief balanced regional model is particularly useful for determining regional implications of national projections; the pure interregional model, for determining national implications of regional projections."[4] The principal applications of interregional input-output models, of both the balanced and pure varieties, are in making regional balance of payments studies and interregional flow studies. In both kinds of studies, the economic system is described in terms of interdependent industries and of interrelated regions.[5]

[3] For an illustration of a balanced regional model, see Wassily Leontief, "Interregional Theory," *Studies in the Structure of the American Economy* (New York: Oxford University Press, 1953), pp. 93–115. An example of a pure interregional model is given by Walter Isard in "Interregional and Regional Input-Output Analysis: A Model of a Space Economy," *The Review of Economics and Statistics*, XXXIII (November 1951), 318–28.

[4] *Op. cit.,* p. 318.

[5] Wassily Leontief in collaboration with Alan Strout, "Multiregional Input-Output Analysis," in Tibor Barna (ed.), *Structural Interdependence and Economic Development* (New York: St. Martin's Press, 1963), p. 119.

Interregional input-output models are more complex than either national or strictly regional models. This is because two kinds of interdependence — interindustrial and interregional — must be blended. One consequence of this complexity is that the interregional input-output tables constructed thus far have been rather highly aggregated. This is not so much because of computational problems, although these are formidable, but rather because the detailed data on industry purchases and sales by region are not available. It has been necessary either to limit the analysis to a few broad regions (e.g. the East, West, and South) or, if a finer regional breakdown is used, to work with rather highly aggregated industrial data. While interregional input-output models are more complex than national or regional models, the basic principles of input-output analysis remain unchanged. The transactions table of such a model shows not only the sales of a given industry to all other industries in the region, but also the sales of that industry to all other industries in the other regions in the system. Figure 4–1 on page 61 illustrates the format of an interregional input-output model. No attempt will be made to work out even a simple illustration. This figure illustrates a "pure" interregional model. If the appropriate data could be obtained for each of the interindustry and interregional transactions, it would be possible to compute input coefficients (as in Table 2–2) for each region. It would then be possible to investigate the implications of changes in final demand for each industry in each region.[6] Economists have had relatively little success in the implementation of such models to date because of the lack of data on interregional shipments. If reliable data were available in the necessary detail, and a table such as the one illustrated could be constructed, this type of interregional model could be very useful. It would show how changes in final demand for the products of one region generate impulses that are transmitted to other regions.

In practice, there has been somewhat more success in implementing balanced interregional models.[7] An interesting variation of a balanced interregional model has been developed by Leon

[6] Isard, *op. cit.*, p. 322.
[7] See for example Walter Isard, "Some Empirical Results and Problems of Regional Input-Output Analysis," in *Studies in the Structure of the American Economy*, pp. 116–81.

FIGURE 4–1

Interregional and Regional Input-Output Table

	East				South				West						Subtotals			
	1. Agriculture & Fishing	2. Food Processing	9. Chemicals	20. Households & Govt	1. Agriculture & Fishing	2. Food Processing	9. Chemicals	20. Households & Govt	1. Agriculture & Fishing	2. Food Processing	9. Chemicals	20. Households & Govt	Exports (national)	Total Output	1. Agriculture & Fishing	2. Food Processing	9. Chemicals	20. Households & Govt
East 1. Agriculture & Fishing																		
2. Food Processing																		
9. Chemicals																		
20. Households & Govt																		
South 1. Agriculture & Fishing																		
2. Food Processing																		
9. Chemicals																		
20. Households & Govt																		
West 1. Agriculture & Fishing																		
2. Food Processing																		
9. Chemicals																		
20. Households & Govt																		
Imports (national)																		
Total Input																		
Subtotals 1. Agriculture & Fishing																		
2. Food Processing																		
9. Chemicals																		
20. Households & Govt																		

Source: Walter Isard, "Interregional and Regional Input-Output Analysis: A Model of a Space Economy," *The Review of Economics and Statistics,* XXXIII (November 1951), 321, Cambridge, Mass.: Harvard University Press, Copyright, 1951, by the President and Fellows of Harvard College.

Moses. He has blended interregional input-output analysis and a linear programming technique to make an empirical study of regional comparative advantage in the United States.[8] This approach has permitted Moses to allow for substitution, and to compute an optimal trade pattern for regional manufacturing.[9] The study by Moses is a pioneering effort, and suggests one interesting direction for further research. The methodology of the study is ingenious and the empirical results are interesting. There are some serious data problems involved in following this approach, however, and these weaken to some extent the empirical findings. These problems will not be discussed at this point, but will be considered in some detail later in this chapter.

An example of a pure interregional model. The examples discussed above are of the type Isard has called balanced interregional models. As Leontief has pointed out, these are models of *intra*national relationships.[10] In the following paragraphs, a different type of interregional model will be described briefly. It is a variation of the pure interregional model developed by Isard. It differs in one important respect, however, from any of the models discussed thus far. All of the models discussed up to now consist of various regions of the *national* economy. The present model, however, is limited to a single region—the Colorado River Basin—but it consists of a series of six input-output tables, one for each of the sub-basins of the larger river basin.[11]

---

[8] Leon N. Moses, "A General Equilibrium Model of Production, Interregional Trade, and Location of Industry," *The Review of Economics and Statistics,* XLII (November 1960), 373–97.

[9] Linear programming is a more recent development than input-output analysis, and may be considered as a lineal descendant of the input-output approach. Input-output analysis as such is not an optimizing technique. It shows what conditions in the economy are rather than what they "ought to be" on the basis of some criterion or set of criteria. Linear programming—a technique which can be applied at the level of the firm, a region, or the national economy—*is* an optimizing technique. In applying linear programming, an *objective function* is set up specifying what is to be maximized or minimized subject to an explicit set of constraints. As Moses has done, it is possible to blend the input-output and linear programming approaches to construct a hybrid optimizing model.

[10] "Interregional Theory," *loc. cit.,* p. 93.

[11] This model was used by the author, in collaboration with Professor Bernard Udis of the University of New Mexico, and Dr. Clyde Stewart, of the Economic Research Service, U. S. Department of Agriculture, as the basis of a comprehensive study of economic growth in the Colorado River Basin conducted for the United States Public Health Service of the U. S. Department of Health,

In this analysis, a separate regional input-output table was constructed for each of the six sub-basins.[12] The sub-basin tables are linked together through import rows and export columns. That is, instead of the single import row and export column found in a national table, each of the sub-basin tables has two import rows and two export columns. One import row, in each of the sub-basin tables, shows imports from other sub-basins in the Colorado River Basin, and the remaining rows show imports from the "rest of the world." Similarly, there is a column showing exports from each sub-basin to all other sub-basins, and a second column for exports outside the Colorado River Basin. Through this linkage it is possible to show how an exogenous change (a change in final demand) in any one sub-basin will affect the level of activity in other sub-basins. Although it is rather an awkward term, this is actually an inter-sub-regional model since it is primarily concerned with intraregional interdependence. It is not, strictly speaking, a regional model of the type to be described in the next section since more than one region is involved.

Each of the sub-basin input-output tables was constructed separately; a table of direct input coefficients (similar to Table 2–2), and one of direct and indirect requirements per dollar of sales to final demand (similar to Table 2–3), were then computed for each of the transactions tables. After the six tables had been constructed independently, the import rows and export columns were reconciled to make the six sub-basin tables internally consistent.

Earlier interregional studies based on a balanced model, such as the one conducted by Moses, have resulted in a large table representing the national economy on a regional basis.[13] No

Education and Welfare. A large staff of graduate research assistants from the University of Colorado and the University of New Mexico, and a number of economists from the Economic Research Service, U. S. Department of Agriculture, collected data for the transactions tables. Mr. John H. Chapman, Jr., and Mrs. Carol Fuller of the Bureau of Economic Research at the University of Colorado were particularly helpful in the construction of the tables and in working out the computational routines.

[12] The sub-basins are natural drainage areas within the larger Colorado River Basin. The latter includes all of the state of Arizona and parts of California, Nevada, Utah, Wyoming, Colorado, and New Mexico.

[13] See Leon N. Moses, "The Stability of Interregional Trading Patterns and Input-Output Analysis," *The American Economic Review*, XLV (December 1955), 814–15.

effort was made to do this in the Colorado River Basin study. It would have been possible to do so, but the separate sub-basin transactions tables are not symmetrical; that is, they do not contain the same number of rows and columns. And because this is a very large region, covering approximately 12 per cent of the land area of the United States, there is considerable specialization of economic activity within each sub-basin. Because of the sheer bulk that would have been involved (approximately a 300×300 table), the sub-basin tables were not put together into a single table for the entire river basin. For analytical purposes, of course, each of the sub-basin tables must be considered as part of the broader interdependent river-basin "table." While the details of this study cannot be reported here it might be noted that an incremental-flow — "dynamic" — model was used in making long-term projections. These then were tied to the future water requirements of the detailed sectors of the Colorado River Basin economy.

Regional Input-Output Analysis

Regional input-output studies differ significantly from the interregional analyses discussed earlier in this chapter. Perhaps a less confusing term is to refer to them as "small-area" input-output studies. The basic model used in small-area studies is similar to that used in the construction of national input-output tables. In most cases, however, variations in the basic national model have been made to suit local circumstances.

Some regional models cover fairly broad geographic areas, such as a Federal Reserve District.[14] Others have been limited to a specific state, a group of counties within a state, a Standard Metropolitan Statistical Area, and at least one study has been concerned with a small community (population under 50,000) which is only a small part of a Standard Metropolitan Statistical Area. Specific reference will be made to some of these studies in the following discussion.

[14] See for example Walter Isard, "Regional Commodity Balances and Interregional Commodity Flows," *The American Economic Review*, XLIII (May 1953), 168–80, a study of the New England Federal Reserve District, and "The Eighth District Balance of Trade," *Monthly Review*, Federal Reserve Bank of St. Louis, XXXIV (June 1952), 69–85.

In general, regional input-output models are more "open" than those which apply to national economies; this is particularly true of regional models in the United States. Compared with any of its regions, the United States economy is quite "closed." International trade (exports plus imports) accounts for a relatively small part of total transactions in this country. There is more specialization and exchange among regions, however, so that regional imports and exports account for a substantial proportion of total transactions.

There are two basic types of regional input-output models which are distinguished by the detail in which imports and exports are recorded in the transactions table. For simplicity, these will be referred to as the "dog-leg" and "square" models. The square model is identical with the national input-output table of the kind illustrated by Table 2–1. While it might contain two or more import rows and a corresponding number of export columns, both imports and exports are highly aggregated in this type of system. In the dog-leg model imports and exports are disaggregated by industry and sector. The basic transactions table of the region being analyzed is set in the upper left-hand corner. This part of the table is similar to a national table except that it does not include an import row and an export column. Instead there is an export "table" appended to the right of the transactions table, and a similar import "table" appended below the transactions table. Such a table shows the interindustry transactions *within* the region and also the detailed interindustry transactions between this region and another region or "the rest of the world."[15]

This type of transactions table is particularly useful for making a structural analysis. It shows in detail the sources of demand for goods and services produced in the region under study, and it shows in similar industrial detail where imports come from and the destination of exports. If one wishes to go beyond a detailed description of structural interrelationships, however, not all of the detail in the dog-leg table can be employed. The only part of the table which is inverted to obtain a table of direct and indirect requirements per dollar of final demand is the processing, or

[15] For illustrations of tables of this kind, see Werner Hochwald, *et al., The Local Impact of Foreign Trade* (Washington: The National Planning Association, 1960); the transactions tables have been published as supplements to this report.

endogenous, sector of the basic region's transactions table. And in practice the final demand columns are combined into a single final demand vector for analytical purposes. When this stage of the analysis is reached, the export and import "tables" are collapsed into a single row and a single column. For most purposes it is not necessary to go into this much industrial detail about imports and exports, and a square transactions table — similar to a national table — is used. The New England and Eighth Federal Reserve District tables mentioned above are of this type, and this is true of all of the state input-output tables with which the author is familiar.

Data Problems in Regional and Interregional Input-Output Analysis

All of the interregional input-output tables constructed in the United States to date and (to the best of the author's knowledge) all of the early regional tables were based upon input coefficients taken from the national table. The procedure in constructing such tables was to obtain (or estimate) total gross output figures for each industry and sector in the region or regions to be analyzed. These figures, for each industry and sector, were then multiplied by *national* input coefficients. The result in each case was a table of interindustry flows *based on the assumption that regional input patterns were identical to national input patterns.* This assumption imposes a severe limitation upon the use of such input-output tables for analytical purposes. It should not be assumed that the economists who used national coefficients to derive regional and interregional commodity flow estimates were unaware of this limitation. The lack of data on a regional basis — particularly of accurate data on shipments from region to region — forced them to turn to this expedient. In his early study of the New England economy, Isard warned that "these input requirements are merely crude estimates."[16]

The major problem involved in using national input coefficients to construct regional tables is that of variations in "industry-mix"

[16]"Regional Commodity Balances and Interregional Commodity Flows," p. 170.

and "product-mix" from region to region. This problem is minimized if a table of national coefficients is available in great detail, but even in this case it is not completely solved. If, for example, the industrial classification used in constructing a national table followed the four-digit Standard Industrial Classification (which, essentially, is at the level of the individual establishment), and if the distribution of industries *within* the region were available in similar detail, the national coefficients might not differ significantly from the regional coefficients. But even the most detailed table published by the U. S. Department of Labor in its 1947 national input-output study—a table which contained 192 rows and columns—was not entirely sufficient for this purpose. The problem is essentially one of industrial classification, or the aggregation problem again.

An important forward step in regional input-output analysis was taken by Moore and Petersen when they constructed their input-output table for Utah. These authors followed Isard's procedure (and that of other early regional input-output analysts) in estimating total gross output figures for the 26 sectors of their transactions table from published sources. Their next step was to use national input coefficients to determine interindustry flows *as a first approximation*. Following this, "the row and column distributions for each sector were modified in the light of differences in regional productive processes, marketing practices, or product-mix."[17] These modifications were based on all the information they could obtain about individual industries, upon technical data, and upon estimates constructed from employment and income data. Such modifications of national input coefficients were feasible in the Utah study, but they could have been used only at great expense in earlier studies covering larger and more densely populated geographic areas. The Moore-Petersen study served as a model for other regional researchers, however, and marked a major step forward in regional input-output analysis. Not only did they depart from the earlier practice of using unadjusted national coefficients in implementing a regional model, but Moore and Petersen made important contributions to the

[17] Frederick T. Moore and James W. Petersen, "Regional Analysis: An Interindustry Model of Utah," *The Review of Economics and Statistics,* XXXVII (November 1955), 371.

development of regional income and employment multipliers. These were discussed in the preceding chapter.

The next major advance in implementing the regional input-output model was made by Werner Z. Hirsch in his study of the St. Louis Metropolitan Area.[18] The input-output study was part of a larger economic investigation of the economy of the St. Louis Metropolitan Area. Hirsch followed the customary practice of obtaining gross output figures, and other "control totals" from published sources. He did not, however, apply national coefficients to these control totals to obtain interindustry flows. Instead, "input and output data were obtained for most large and medium sized companies operating in the St. Louis area . . . each of these companies assigned one of its key officials to work with the research staff of this study for a three-months' period. Each company prepared its own input-output table for 1955."[19] The participants in the study were carefully briefed orally and given written instructions to ensure uniformity of reporting. Where only a sample of firms in an industry was included in the survey, the sample results were "blown up" on the basis of employment data. Once the interindustry flows had been established, the aggregated results could be compared with control totals obtained from published data, and the necessary reconciliations were made. The St. Louis transactions table is of the dog-leg variety discussed above, which gives detailed import and export flows as well as interindustry flows within the St. Louis area.

While the method employed by Hirsch is expensive and time-consuming, there is little doubt about its superiority to other estimating techniques. One of the major criticisms of regional input-output analysis, made before Hirsch published the results of his study, was that of using national coefficients at the regional level.[20] By using primary data Hirsch avoided this criticism. But

---

[18]Werner Z. Hirsch, "Interindustry Relations of a Metropolitan Area," *The Review of Economics and Statistics*, XLI (November 1959), 360–69. The transactions table is given as an appendix in John C. Bollens, *Exploring the Metropolitan Community* (Berkeley and Los Angeles: University of California Press, 1961), pp. 460–71; an excellent discussion of methodology and further information about data sources are given in pages 369–87.

[19]*Ibid.*, p. 361.

[20]Charles M. Tiebout, "Regional and Interregional Input-Output Models: An Appraisal," *The Southern Economic Journal*, XXIV (October 1957), 143–44.

it must be emphasized that the more accurate input coefficients derived from the St. Louis table were obtained only at relatively high cost.

Since publication of the Moore-Petersen and Hirsch studies, few regional input-output studies have relied upon national input coefficients. For one thing, by the late 1950s it was recognized that the 1947 national input coefficients could no longer be used without major adjustments. Some of the more recent studies have used the Moore-Petersen approach of applying adjusted national coefficients to state or regional control totals. Others, however, have followed Hirsch's lead in conducting surveys to obtain estimates of interindustry flows. This procedure was followed, for example, in the Colorado River Basin Study mentioned above.

Regional Impact Analyses

As noted earlier, *interregional* input-output models have been used primarily for the study of regional balance of payments and interregional trade flows. The primary use of *regional* models, however, has been in making local or regional impact studies.

Local and regional impact studies are designed to measure the direct, indirect, and induced income and employment effects of changes in final demand in one or more sectors of the local or regional economy. This is done by computing income and employment multipliers as discussed in Chapter 3. As noted in that chapter, most multiplier studies have been regional in nature. This is also true of most impact analyses.[21] Indeed, the only difference between an impact analysis and a general multiplier analysis is that in the former attention is focused on the total changes in an economy (national or regional) which are expected to result from exogenous changes—changes in final demand in some of the major sectors of an input-output system. Most regional impact studies have been concerned with measuring the effects of changes in final demand for existing industries in the region. Some, however, have been concerned with measurement of the total impact

[21] A major exception is the study by Wassily W. Leontief and Marvin Hoffenberg, "The Economic Effects of Disarmament," *Scientific American,* CCIV (April 1961), 3–11.

of the location of a new industry in an area. The Isard-Kuenne study discussed in Chapter 3 is an example of the latter.

Other Uses of Regional Input-Output Analysis

State Economic Development programs. Input-output as a development tool will be discussed more fully in the next chapter. It is mentioned at this point, however, since one of the more recent applications of regional input-output methods in the United States has been in connection with state economic development programs. Almost every state has some form of economic development organization which has the responsibility for stimulating local economic initiative, and in some cases for luring business establishments — especially manufacturing plants — from other areas. Most state organizations of this kind have large advertising budgets, and their principal activity is that of publicizing the economic advantages of their state (real or imagined). It is difficult to judge the effectiveness of such advertising, but it has been one of the major approaches followed in "area development."

In recent years, however, some state development organizations have adopted a more analytic approach in an effort to use their resources more effectively. By means of locational analysis they are trying to identify the types of economic activity best suited to their areas. Some have been interested in identifying activities with high income and employment multipliers. Regional input-output analysis is ideally suited for the latter purpose.

The Mississippi Industrial Development Commission, for example, has constructed an input-output table for the state, and from this it has derived a "self-sufficiency" chart. Such a chart (described and illustrated in the next chapter) shows the economic activities within the state which produce a surplus for export, and the principal products and services which are imported. The chart is an effective and useful development tool. It shows at a glance the local markets which might be served by new establishments. No state development organization actually hopes to make the state's economy self-sufficient. By substituting analysis for the earlier "butterfly-net" approach to industrial recruitment, however, the development organization is able to apply its energies and resources in the directions which promise to yield the greatest returns.

With a state input-output table it is possible to show the *total* income and employment impacts which new industries will have upon a state. This can be done by inserting a new row and column in the table using input coefficients from other regional models (or if necessary estimates based upon a national model), and by deriving a new matrix of direct and indirect requirements per dollar of sales to final demand (Table 2–3). In a similar way it is possible to measure the income and employment effects of the expansion of existing economic activities.

State and regional consistent forecasting. Another use of state and regional input-output models is in making consistent forecasts. This procedure has already been described for the national model, and it need not be repeated here. There are some special problems of consistent regional forecasting, however, which will be discussed briefly.

One of the major differences between regional economies and the economy of the United States is that the former are much more "open" than the latter. That is, imports and exports account for a larger proportion of total transactions in a region than in the nation. Interregional "imports and exports" cancel out when a national input-output table is constructed.

In making long-range consistent forecasts at the regional level, the effects of changes in relative prices and technical coefficients must be taken into account as in the case of national consistent forecast. Much more attention must be paid to the effects of changing trade patterns on a region's input coefficients than in the national case, however. This can be illustrated by a simple example.

Assume that in a base period, a region relies heavily upon some extractive activity – say the mining of coal and various minerals. At one stage of the region's development both the coal and ore might be shipped to other regions. Since ore is in general a "weight-losing" material, however, at some point it will become economical to locate a concentrating mill close to the mines. The minerals will then become an input to the concentrating mill, and only the metal concentrate will be exported. If the production of this ore expands, however, it might soon become economical to locate a smelter in the region. The concentrate will then no longer be an export, but will become an input to the smelter. The smelter, in turn, could stimulate the growth of various types of fabricating operations in the area, and these might attract satellite activities. The location of a smelter and of fabricating activities in the region would change the distribution pattern of coal mined in the area. The smelter would use coal as inputs, and this might also be true of some of the fabricating plants, so that relatively less coal would show up in the export column as some part of regional production became inputs to establishments in the area.

Because there is more specialization in regional economies than in the national economy, such changes in trade patterns can have a rather large effect upon technical coefficients. This does not mean that consistent forecasting at the regional level is hopeless. What it does mean is that the regional forecaster, using an input-output model, must rely heavily upon location theory and a careful study of economic development when making long-range projections. It might be necessary to insert a number of new rows and columns in a projected table based upon an analysis of the most probable path of development. In some cases the analysis of time series might show what to expect. In others the forecaster might have to rely upon location theory to suggest agglomeration patterns which could significantly alter the structure of the regional economy. There has been relatively little empirical work of this kind, but because of the potential usefulness of consistent forecasting to businessmen and policy-makers in specific regions it is likely that such activity will increase. At present, consistent regional forecasts are likely to provide only rough and broad guidelines. Hopefully, further research on dynamic input-output analysis will lead to the development of models which could provide more accurate and longer-range consistent regional forecasts.

A Variation of Regional Input-Output Analysis — "Rows Only"

Regional analysts interested in constructing an input-output table have been faced with the choice of either applying national coefficients to control totals for the region or of collecting the necessary data on interindustry transactions by means of a detailed survey. The first approach suffers from a number of defects. The industry-mix for a typical region is likely to be such that national coefficients will provide only the crudest approximations to interindustry flows for the region. The second approach (in addition to the statistical hazards involved in any survey) is expensive. Economists do not, or should not, undertake a regional input-output study lightly or without adequate financing.

In an effort to find a middle ground between these two problems, a variation of the regional input-output system, called an *intersectoral flows model,* was developed by Charles M. Tiebout and his associates at the University of California at Los Angeles.[22] The intersectoral flows model has been dubbed the "rows only" approach to interindustry analysis. The model incorporates some of the features of an economic base-multiplier approach as well as some of the features of regional input-output analysis. The primary difference between the intersectoral flows model and a full-scale regional input-output model is that in implementing the former model a sample of firms were "asked . . . to break down a typical dollar of their 1960 sales to various final demand sectors or to local industry groups. *No information on inputs was requested."*[23] Information on the distribution of sales was obtained from manufacturing firms by means of a mail questionnaire. Data for nonmanufacturing establishments were obtained from published sources plus interviews with a limited number of firms and discussions with industry experts.

In implementing a regional input-output model as opposed to the intersectoral flows model, the typical procedure is to conduct interviews with sample firms in each industry and sector to obtain data on *both* inputs and sales. After the sample data have been aggregated and "blown up" to cover all transactions (by using control totals from published sources) there remains the problem of reconciling differences between the input and output data. This

[22] See W. Lee Hansen and Charles M. Tiebout, "An Intersectoral Flows Analysis of the California Economy," *The Review of Economics and Statistics,* XLV (November 1963), 409–18. See also W. Lee Hansen, R. Thayne Robson, and Charles M. Tiebout, *Markets for California Products* (Sacramento, California: State of California Economic Development Agency, 1961).

[23] Hansen and Tiebout, *op. cit.,* p. 411; emphasis added.

involves a substantial amount of clerical work plus the exercise of informed judgment. The sample surveys generally are both time-consuming and expensive, even for a relatively small area. And the statistical problems of reconciling input and output data add to the cost of a full-scale regional input-output analysis. These problems are avoided in the intersectoral flows model which uses output (sales) data only. Since the data are arranged in the form of an input-output table, the model implicitly assumes that the columns represent inputs. If businessmen will cooperate in completing mail questionnaires, an intersectoral flows model can be implemented at a much lower cost than a full-scale regional input-output table. In the view of Tiebout and his associates, this is one of the major advantages of their approach.

There is another major difference between the intersectoral flows model and a regional input-output table. In the input-output table, all transactions are expressed in dollar terms. In the intersectoral flows model, however, data on employment were entered in the basic table which is analogous to a transactions table (such as Table 2–1). From this point on, the intersectoral flows model utilized the same procedures as a regional input-output model. Input coefficients were developed, but these were expressed in terms of employment rather than dollar transactions.

The objective of the intersectoral flows model was to measure sectoral employment multipliers. In the study by Tiebout and his associates, the employment input coefficients show the amount of California employment required in industry A to satisfy the demand for A's output by all other industries and sectors in the system. The method of computing the employment multipliers is similar to that used by Isard and Kuenne in their impact study. That is, the direct employment effects were first estimated and then the indirect effects were computed by an iterative process which measured the second, third, and succeeding "rounds" of employment impacts. By repeatedly carrying out the process of iteration, "all employment originally assigned to local industries can be assigned indirectly to the . . . final demand sectors."[24]

Partisans of regional input-output analysis might point out that the standard regional input-output model can provide employment multipliers as well as a considerable amount of additional

[24] *Ibid.*, p. 416.

information. But they would have to admit that a full-scale regional input-output table would be far more costly. As Hansen and Tiebout have pointed out, "the most obvious advantage of the [intersectoral flows analysis] lies in its operational simplicity. Although other approaches may have certain advantages at the conceptual level, the real problem is one of generating the necessary data at a reasonable cost and on a recurrent basis so that regional economies can be more fully analyzed."[25]

Conclusions

There have been relatively few empirical interregional input-output studies. The major problem has been one of a lack of data. The major data deficiency is that of interregional commodity and money flows. As an expedient, analysts have been forced to use national coefficients to estimate regional input patterns. There have been a number of methodological advances in interregional input-output analysis in recent years, but the major barrier to their empirical implementation has been the high costs which would be involved.

A large number of regional input-output studies have been completed in recent years, however, and a number of others are under way. Early regional input-output tables, like their interregional counterparts, were based on national input coefficients. Since the pioneering work of Werner Hirsch, however, there has been a tendency for data on interindustry transactions and sales to final demand to be obtained by means of interviews. Those who have engaged in this type of research acknowledge that it is time-consuming and expensive. They feel that the results justify the efforts and costs involved, however. The most recent development has been the intersectoral flows analysis, or "rows only" approach discussed in the preceding section. This approach has its limitations, but it has one major advantage—it can be empirically implemented at reasonable cost. There has been growing interest in regional input-output analysis in recent years, and as in any other area of research, this activity should lead to the development of new concepts and to the refinement of statistical techniques for the implementation of input-output models.

[25] *Ibid.*, p. 418.

REFERENCES

BOLLENS, JOHN C., *Exploring the Metropolitan Community* (Berkeley and Los Angeles: University of California Press, 1961).

CLELAND, SHERRILL, "Local Input-Output Analysis: A New Business Tool," *Business Topics,* Michigan State University, VII (Autumn 1959), 41–48.

FREUTEL, GUY, "The Eighth District Balance of Trade," *Monthly Review,* Federal Reserve Bank of St. Louis, XXXIV (June 1952), 69–78.

HANSEN, W. LEE, R. THAYNE ROBSON and CHARLES M. TIEBOUT, *Markets for California Products* (Sacramento: State of California Economic Development Agency, 1961).

——— and CHARLES M. TIEBOUT, "An Intersectoral Flows Analysis of the California Economy," *The Review of Economics and Statistics,* XLV (November 1963), 409–18.

HIRSCH, WERNER Z., "An Application of Area Input-Output Analysis," *Papers and Proceedings,* The Regional Science Association, V (1959), 79–92.

———, "Interindustry Relations of a Metropolitan Area," *The Review of Economics and Statistics,* XLI (November 1959), pp. 360–69.

HOCHWALD, WERNER, "Sources and Uses of Eighth District Funds in 1952," *Monthly Review,* Federal Reserve Bank of St. Louis, XXXV (May 1953), 49–59.

———, HERBERT E. STRINER and SYDNEY SONENBLUM, *Local Impact of Foreign Trade* (Washington, D.C.: National Planning Association, 1960). This report is supplemented by a series of mimeographed reports dealing with methodology and sources of data. The transactions table for the three areas analyzed as part of the Local Impact of Foreign Trade (LIFT) study are also available as supplements.

ISARD, WALTER, "Interregional and Regional Input-Output Analysis: A Model of a Space-Economy," *The Review of Economics and Statistics,* XXXIII (November 1951), pp. 318–28.

———, "Regional Commodity Balances and Interregional Commodity Flows," *American Economic Review,* XLIII (May 1953), pp. 167–80.

———, "Some Empirical Results and Problems of Regional Input-Output Analysis," in Wassily Leontief, *et al., Studies in the Structure of the American Economy* (New York: Oxford University Press, 1953), pp. 116–81.

——— and ROBERT E. KUENNE, "The Impact of Steel Upon the Greater New York–Philadelphia Industrial Region," *The Review of Economics and Statistics,* XXXV (November 1953), 289–301.

LEONTIEF, WASSILY, "Interregional Theory," in Leontief, *et al., Studies in the Structure of the American Economy* (New York: Oxford University Press, 1953), pp. 93–115.

_____ in collaboration with ALAN STROUT, "Multiregional Input-Output Analysis," in Tibor Barna (ed.), *Structural Interdependence and Economic Development* (New York: St. Martin's Press, 1963), pp. 119–50.

MIERNYK, WILLIAM H., ERNEST BONNER, JOHN H. CHAPMAN, JR., and KENNETH SHELLHAMMER, *The Impact of Space and Space-Related Activities on a Local Community: Part I, The Input-Output Analysis,* report submitted to the National Aeronautics and Space Administration (July 1965).

MILLER, RONALD E., "Impact of the Aluminum Industry on the Pacific Northwest: A Regional Input-Output Analysis," *The Review of Economics and Statistics,* XXXIX (May 1953), 200–9.

MOORE, FREDERICK T., "Regional Economic Reaction Paths," *American Economic Review,* XLV (May 1955), 133–48. Discussions by Phillip Neff and Leon Moses, 149–53.

_____ and JAMES W. PETERSEN, "Regional Analysis: An Interindustry Model of Utah," *Review of Economics and Statistics,* XXXVII (November 1955), 368–81.

MOSES, LEON N., "A General Equilibrium Model of Production, Interregional Trade and Location of Industry," *The Review of Economics and Statistics,* XLII (November 1960), 373–97.

_____, "The Stability of Interregional Trading Patterns and Input-Output Analysis," *The American Economic Review,* XLV (December 1955), 803–32.

STEVENS, BENJAMIN H., "A Review of the Literature on Linear Methods and Models for Spatial Analysis," *Journal of the American Institute of Planners,* XXVI (August 1960), 253–59.

TIEBOUT, CHARLES M., "Regional and Interregional Input-Output Models: An Appraisal," *The Southern Economic Journal,* XXIV (November 1957), 140–47.

5 International Developments

The first government agency to undertake the construction of a full-scale national input-output table was the Bureau of Labor Statistics of the Department of Labor. This effort resulted in the publication of a 50-sector table of interindustry relations in the United States and of a much more detailed 200-sector table with finer industrial and sectoral classifications.[1] The hypothetical table described in Chapter 2 (Table 2–1) is modeled after the 1947 national table published by the Bureau of Labor Statistics. To construct this table, a separate Division of Interindustry Economics had been established in the Bureau of Labor Statistics. An important result of this early work in input-output analysis was a projection of the U.S. economy to 1950.[2]

The work of the Division of Interindustry Economics attracted widespread attention among economists and businessmen. Unfortunately, in some quarters it was considered "controversial." Some businessmen were said to have viewed the program as a step toward "push button planning" and a threat to private enterprise.[3] Appropriations to the Department of Labor were curtailed and, while the Department of Defense had sufficient funds to continue work on input-output analysis, the decision was made by a Deputy Secretary of Defense to terminate support of input-output studies after November 1953.[4] There was no further work

[1] For an excellent discussion of the 50-sector table, see W. Duane Evans and Marvin Hoffenberg, "The Interindustry Relations Study for 1947," *The Review of Economics and Statistics,* XXXIV (May 1952), 97–142. See also *General Explanations of the 200 Sector Tables: The 1947 Interindustry Relations Study* (United States Department of Labor, BLS Report No. 33, June 1953).

[2] Jerome Cornfield, W. Duane Evans, and Marvin Hoffenberg, *Full Employment Patterns, 1950* (U.S. Department of Labor, Bureau of Labor Statistics, Serial No. R. 1868, 1947), reprinted from the February and March issues of the *Monthly Labor Review.*

[3] *Business Week* (August 29, 1953), 26.   [4] *Ibid.*

on interindustry analysis by the United States government until after the Census of Manufactures of 1958. At that time, the Office of Business Economics of the U.S. Department of Commerce undertook the construction of a new input-output table for 1958 which was published toward the end of 1964.

Research on input-output analysis continued at the Harvard Economic Research Project and at other universities, largely financed by foundation funds. But the construction of a national input-output table is a major statistical effort. While private research organizations are admirably suited to conduct *research* on input-output analysis, and in many cases to conduct regional input-output studies, the statistical and financial resources of government agencies appear to be a prerequisite for the successful construction of national tables. And because of the curtailment of funds in 1953, there was a period of more than five years during which government agencies in the United States could not engage in such analysis.

Although empirical work on input-output analysis languished in the United States, it surged ahead in other countries. And the rapid spread of input-output analysis throughout the world stimulated a large number of theoretical studies to complement the empirical work being done. By 1961, a *partial* bibliography of input-output studies — both empirical and theoretical — published by the United Nations ran to 222 pages, and agencies in about 40 countries were involved in interindustry studies.

As early as 1951 there was sufficient interest in this new analytic technique to stimulate an international conference on interindustrial relations. This conference, which met in Driebergen, Holland, brought together economists interested in the theoretical, the statistical, and the computational problems of interindustry analysis.[5] A second conference was held between June 27 and July 10, 1954, at Varenna, Italy.[6] A third international conference was held in September 1961 in Geneva. Economists and statisticians from more than 41 different countries participated in this conference. For the first time, representatives of the

[5]The Netherlands Economic Institute, *Input-Output Relations,* Proceedings of the Conference on Interindustrial Relations held at Driebergen, Holland (Leiden 1953).

[6]Tibor Barna (ed.), *The Structural Interdependence of the Economy,* Proceedings of an International Conference on Input-Output Analysis (New York and Milan: John Wiley & Sons, Inc., and A. Giuffre, 1956).

Soviet Union and of other socialist countries, as well as planners from underdeveloped countries, participated in the international input-output conference.[7]

The first international conference dealt largely with the empirical implementation of input-output systems. The major emphasis of the second conference was on statistical and computational procedures and problems. The central theme of the third conference was the application of input-output analysis to projection and developmental planning.[8] Thus, during the decade spanning the three international conferences, there was a marked shift from emphasis on the problems of constructing input-output systems to the *application* of these systems to a variety of economic problems.

Input-Output Analysis in Planned and Unplanned Economies

The first empirical application of input-output analysis was in the United States, an unplanned economy which depends upon market forces for the allocation of resources and the distribution of income. The input-output system is not a tool developed by "planners" with the intent of substituting another form of economic organization for the market system. Indeed, the early work in interindustry analysis was oriented toward a market economy. The objective was to measure, as precisely as possible, the impact upon the economy of *autonomous* changes in final demand. Within the framework of a free-market economy, the input-output analyst is not particularly concerned about the causes of changes in final demand. These are "given." And once they have been estimated, the input-output system will show the levels of activity which will have to be met within the endogenous sectors to sustain this level of final demand. The input-output system as such is not a planning tool — *it is an analytical tool.* But while it was developed within the framework of a market economy, it soon became apparent that this tool could be applied to other types of economy systems as well.

[7] Tibor Barna (ed.), *Structural Interdependence and Economic Development,* Proceedings of an International Conference on Input-Output Techniques, Geneva, September 1961 (New York: St. Martin's Press, 1963).

[8] From the preface by Wassily Leontief to *Structural Interdependence and Economic Development,* p. v.

Input-output analysis in partially planned economies. Before World War II, there was considerable debate among economists about the virtues of "planned" versus "unplanned" economies. Much of this debate was conducted in polar terms. One either talked about a "planned" economy, by which one meant a *totally* planned economy (of which the Soviet Union was generally considered the prototype), or one talked about an "unplanned" economy by which was usually meant a laissez-faire system in which all economic decisions were made by the invisible hand of the market place.

Experience since the end of World War II has shown that much of this debate was of purely academic interest. Like so many controversies which pose two absolute conditions as mutually exclusive alternatives, this one was shown to be of relatively little relevance to the real world. During the second world war, there was a great deal of "planning" in all of the countries which participated in the hostilities. And after the war, many of the countries in Western Europe continued to engage in what might be called "partial" planning. This type of planning may or may not be associated with some degree of socialism — some degree of government ownership and operation of the major means of production (usually basic "heavy" industries). In Great Britain, for example, the government nationalized some industries; in other cases, such as France and Italy, there was little or no experimentation with socialism, but in these and other countries there were, and continue to be, various experiments with different kinds of "planning."

The notion of "indicative planning" as it is practiced in France was introduced in Chapter 3 as part of the discussion of consistent forecasting. France is one of the countries whose government has engaged in a certain amount of economic planning in recent years within the framework of a private-enterprise economy. One of the analytical tools which has been prominent in French indicative (or noncoercive) planning is an input-output model which is geared to the French system of national accounts. Long-term projections (five to ten years) of final demand are made, assuming several different rates of growth. These projections provide a set of production targets which will have to be met if the final demand figures are to be realized.

The General Commission on the Plan has the basic responsibility for the initial forecast. Other government agencies also participate. The initial plan is then submitted to committees (e.g. the Committee on General Manufacturing Industries) made up of private businessmen. The committees, which include a few civil servants and trade unionists but are predominantly made up of businessmen, review the plan.

In general, the committees examine the sectoral projections, which are quite aggregated in the French input-output system. They then attempt to determine the detailed industrial outputs which will be required to meet these aggregated projections. At this stage there is still a considerable amount of flexibility in the procedure. Reports are submitted to the General Commissioner for the French plan, and on the basis of these reports the Commissioner may alter the initial projections before the Plan becomes "official." Before this is done, however, the Plan is reviewed by the Economic and Social Council; it is then sent to Parliament. Following this, the official Plan is published, but it *"does not imply any obligation, nor any sanction."*[9]

There is, of course, more to indicative planning in France than this sketchy description suggests. Demographic trends, fiscal policy, the international balance of trade and payments, and other factors are taken into consideration in the preparation of the Plan. The input-output technique, however, is the central analytical tool in French indicative planning. It is also important to stress that in making the long-term projections there is close cooperation between government agencies and committees made up predominantly of private businessmen. The businessmen have recognized that the reduction of uncertainty contributes to the stability of their operations. The effectiveness of this joint action is demonstrated by the rapid growth of the French economy in recent years, and the extent to which "full" employment has been maintained. As is true of most of the industrial nations of Western Europe, France has had a remarkably low unemployment rate in recent years. This is not a suggestion that indicative planning

[9] Felix de Clinchamps, "The Role of Private Enterprise in the Preparation of the Plan," *French and Other National Economic Plans for Growth,* European Committee for Economic and Social Progress (CEPES) (New York: Committee for Economic Development, 1963), p. 62.

is a panacea for all of the ills of industrial society. The only point to be made here is that the input-output system has proved an extremely useful analytical tool in a partially planned economy. It should be noted in conclusion that European nations which have engaged in relatively little "planning" (such as Italy) as well as others which have engaged in more "planning" than France (such as Great Britain) have made extensive use of input-output analysis.[10]

Input-output analysis in a completely planned economy. There is no such thing as a totally planned economy in which every transaction is projected in advance. There is, however, *central* planning; the leading practitioner of this method of allocating resources and distributing income is the Soviet Union. Much of the controversy referred to earlier in this chapter about "planned" versus "unplanned" economies centered on the question: Can economic planning work?

The experience of the Soviet Union shows that central economic planning *can* work, although to an economist trained in the Western tradition the success of early Russian economic planning remains something of a mystery. The basic problem faced by policy-makers in Russia after the Revolution of 1917 was that there were no planning guidelines for the type of system they were trying to set up. The only economic theory tolerated in the Soviet Union was Marxism, and as Leontief has pointed out, "Marxism, as an economic theory, is a theory of rampant private enterprise, not of the centrally guided economy."[11] Nevertheless, under Stalin a series of five-year plans were promulgated, and whether or not the planned targets were achieved, the Russian economy entered an era of rapid growth. The basic principles guiding the early "planners" in the Soviet Union were simple. The objective was to produce as much as possible, consume as little as necessary, and use the surplus for

[10] See Hollis B. Chenery and Paul G. Clark, *Interindustry Economics* (New York: John Wiley & Sons, Inc., 1959), pp. 251–67, and Hollis B. Chenery, Paul G. Clark, and V. Cao-Pinna, *The Structure and Growth of the Italian Economy* (Rome: U.S. Mutual Security Agency, 1953). See also "The ABC of Input-Output," reprinted from the (London) *Economist* (September 19 and 26, 1953) by St. Clements Press, Ltd., and Input-Output Tables for the United Kingdom (London: H.M.S.O., 1961).

[11] Wassily Leontief, "The Decline and Rise of Soviet Economic Science," *Foreign Affairs,* XXXVIII (January 1960), 262.

investment to stimulate further economic growth. Investment decisions (how much to invest and where) were made by Gosplan, the central planning agency. It was this agency which decided investment priorities and production targets after consultation with directors of the major Soviet enterprises. All this was done without a basic analytical model and "so far as the Russian technique of economic planning is concerned, one can apply to it in paraphrase what was said about a talking horse: the remarkable thing about it is not what it says, but that it speaks at all."[12]

Part of the problem faced by Soviet planners was that they were the victims of severe ideological constraints. During the Stalin era, the only economic theory they could use was that of Karl Marx. And while Marx had many penetrating insights about the operation of the capitalist economy, he did nothing to suggest how a centrally planned socialist economy would operate. More recently, however, some of the restraints upon Soviet economists have been lifted; it has been possible for them to study the analytical techniques developed in the West, and to begin to apply them to problems of Soviet economic planning. Until a few years ago, all references to "bourgeois economics" were highly critical. Leontief credits Oskar Lange, formerly a University of Chicago economist and now head of economic planning in Poland, with the introduction of a positive approach to econometrics in the Soviet Union and its satellites.[13] To some extent, however, the new attitude toward analytical tools developed in the West is probably part of the "new freedom" which intellectuals in the Soviet Union have found in the post-Stalin era.

There has been a great deal of interest among Russian economists in input-output analysis in recent years. American books and articles on interindustry analysis have been translated and widely circulated. As they have done in a number of other cases when they have "borrowed" ideas from the West, Russian apologists claimed priority in the invention of input-output analysis. This claim is based upon the publication of an article in a Russian economic journal written by Leontief while he was a student

---

[12] *Ibid.,* 263.

[13] See his *Introduction to Econometrics,* 2nd rev. ed. (New York: The Macmillan Company, 1963), pp. 9–23. More than half of this book is devoted to input-output analysis and the related technique of linear programming.

in Germany.[14] A more legitimate claim to a related technique was found in the earlier-neglected, pioneering work of L. V. Kantorovich.[15] The early paper by Leontief and Kantorovich's work established the intellectual respectability of input-output analysis in the Soviet Union. While empirical work on input-output analysis in Russia lags behind that in a number of other countries, it is apparent that rapid strides are being made.

A great deal of secrecy surrounds the work on input-output analysis in the Soviet Union, but enough information has leaked out to permit the reconstruction of a 38-sector interindustry table for that country based on 1959 transactions.[16] A number of scholars have analyzed Soviet interindustry relations on the basis of partial data released by the Russian government. Recently, for example, Herbert S. Levine has contrasted the ways in which input-output analysis is used in centrally planned and in free-market economies.[17] Somewhat more detailed information about Soviet input-output analysis (as well as the reconstruction of the 1959 Soviet input-output table) are contained in a paper entitled "Economic Interrelations in the Soviet Union," published by the Joint Economic Committee of the U.S. Congress.[18] These studies show that while Soviet input-output analysis is closely patterned after earlier work conducted in the free-market economies, there are some significant differences. These are principally differences in application rather than construction, and to highlight them it will be necessary to give a brief discussion of the Soviet planning process.[19]

[14] The paper was first published in Germany, but was later translated for publication in Russia. See "The Decline and Rise of Soviet Economic Science," *op. cit.*, pp. 269. See also "Soviet Planners Bootleg Western-Style Economics," *Business Week* (June 13, 1959), 92–96.

[15] L. V. Kantorovich, "Mathematical Methods of Organizing and Planning Production," *Management Science*, VI (July 1960), 366–422 (translated by Robert W. Campbell and H. W. Marlow).

[16] Joint Economic Committee, Congress of the United States, *Annual Economic Indicators for the U.S.S.R.* (Washington: U. S. Government Printing Office, 1964), pp. 185–218. This is a summary of a study "Soviet 1959 Interindustry Model: Reconstruction and Analysis," prepared for the Research Analysis Corporation, McLean, Virginia, by Dr. Vladimir G. Treml of Franklin and Marshall College.

[17] Herbert S. Levine, "Input-Output Analysis and Soviet Planning," *American Economic Review*, LII (May 1962), 127–37.

[18] Joint Economic Committee, *op. cit.*

[19] For a more complete discussion see the lucid presentation by Levine, *op. cit.*, pp. 128–31.

The construction of a short-term (annual) plan involves a series of stages. The initial stage consists of what Levine has called the "flow and counterflow of instructions and information." This is followed by establishment of the major objectives of the economy which are given to Gosplan by the nation's political leaders. Gosplan then details a series of preliminary production targets called "control figures." These targets are transmitted through the economic chain of command to the basic enterprises in the Soviet system. Having been given its production target, each enterprise then prepares a list of the material inputs it will need. The enterprise is not free to determine its inputs arbitrarily, but relates them to a set of "materials input norms" most of which are determined at higher levels of the economic chain of command.

In drawing up the plan there are two sets of pressures at work. Those at the top of the planning hierarchy apply pressure to reduce input requirements. At the level of the enterprise, which is responsible for meeting a production quota, there are counterpressures to add a little extra to actual input requirements.

After the initial production targets and input requirements have been prepared, it is up to Gosplan to achieve an internal balance for the plan as a whole, to see that the output targets and the input requirements are consistent. To achieve this, Gosplan uses what has been called the "method of material balances." Essentially, this consists of setting up a series of accounts — similar to the balance sheet used by accountants in a free-market economy, but expressed in terms of materials rather than monetary units. On one side the sources of supply of materials are listed, and the other side lists the uses to which these materials are to be put. As Levine has noted, "it is only by the wildest chance that the two will be equal at the first balancing."[20] In general, the material demands will be greater than the available supplies. It is up to Gosplan to bring the demand and supply into balance, keeping in mind the production targets which have been given the highest priority by the nation's political leaders. Gosplan tries to work out the balance by a trial-and-error approach, or in more technical terms by following an iterative procedure.

[20] *Ibid.*, p. 130.

Even with this sketchy discussion it should be clear why input-output analysis has appealed to Soviet planning technicians. Given a detailed input-output table, Soviet planners could achieve an internal balance very quickly by using electronic computers. Input-output analysis can be conducted in "a language the computer can understand (something not accomplished by the material balances method)."[21] As Levine has noted, much Soviet discussion of input-output analysis has emphasized the speed with which it can be accomplished. In a centrally planned system this is very important since it would permit the development of a *series* of plans from which the Soviet leaders could choose rather than the "often poorly balanced, late, single variant now constructed."[22]

The major difference between the application of input-output analysis in a free-market economy and in a centrally planned economy can now be made explicit. In a free-market economy the input-output analysis generally starts with a set of final demands. Then, given an inverse matrix (the table of direct and indirect coefficients), total outputs can be computed for each sector. By relating these to the table of direct input coefficients, a new table of interindustry transactions for all processing sectors can be constructed.

In a centrally planned economy the targets established are not final demands but *total outputs*. These include not only the final demands but also the interindustry transactions needed to achieve these final uses. It has also been suggested that in a centrally planned economy the input coefficients should not be empirically determined (as in a free-market economy) but that intersectoral balances should be based "on scientifically determined progressive input coefficients."[23]

Up to now Soviet economic planners have used input-output tables based on empirically determined input coefficients, and for short-term planning they have assumed that most of these coefficients will remain stable. Treml has noted that "out of 4,260 input coefficients shown in the 1959 intersectoral balance only 500 were adjusted when the first planning balance was being prepared for 1962."[24] It is evident, however, that some Soviet econ-

[21] *Ibid.*, p. 132.

[22] *Ibid.*, p. 133.

[23] Treml, *op. cit.*, p. 192.

[24] *Ibid.*, p. 185.

omists are thinking in terms of projected coefficients—a goal similar to that of input-output researchers in the Western world who are working on dynamic models.

Input-output tables have also been constructed for a number of other planned economies. By 1964, most of the large countries in the Soviet bloc had prepared such tables. These include Yugoslavia, Poland, Hungary, East Germany, Bulgaria, Czechoslovakia, and Romania.[25] In spite of this impressive array of input-output tables in planned economies, both the theoretical and empirical work on input-output analysis in these countries lags behind that of the Western world. Since economists in the planned economies started to experiment with input-output much later than their counterparts in free-market countries, their accomplishments "should be viewed against the background of ideological obstacles and resistance to change from many quarters."[26]

A Value-Free Science of Economics

Mathematicians and many kinds of physical scientists, such as physicists and chemists, work in areas which are essentially free of political ideology. They can use the same tools, and converse in the same language, whether they live in a society with a free-market or a centrally planned economy. This has not been true in other disciplines, notably the social and biological sciences. It is not surprising, given the antithesis between communism and capitalism, that Soviet leaders would repudiate the entire body of economic theory from the Classical through the Keynesian schools. Indeed, as Leontief has noted, Soviet planners have operated without a theoretical framework since even Marxism is a theory of capitalism which contains no useful guides to the Soviet planner.

The input-output model is independent of political, social, and economic systems. Unlike the models of the major schools of economic thought of the past it says nothing about how resources should be allocated and incomes distributed. It is a value-free

[25] *Ibid.*, p. 188.   [26] *Ibid.*

system which can be applied in free-market, partially planned, or totally planned economies. An input-output analysis tells us nothing about what *should* be; it describes the economy as it is. Various assumptions can be made about changes in technical coefficients, in final demand, or in total gross output. Once these assumptions have been made, the system can be used to make projections regardless of whether resource allocation and income distribution are determined by market forces or executive decree.

As noted, input-output analysis had to become ideologically acceptable before it could be used by economists in the Soviet Union. But this was due entirely to pressures exerted by political leaders; it had nothing to do with the objective reality of input-output analysis. Once the ideological barrier had been hurdled it was still necessary for Soviet economists to reconcile input-output analysis and Marxian theory. According to Marx, the total output of an economy consists of three parts: (1) the value of capital used up in a given period (which is considered to be "embodied labor value"), designated by the symbol c, (2) v which is the value of labor used in the production process, and (3) m which is "surplus value" or profit. The nation's total output therefore equals $c + v + m$.

Although Western economists would not accept such a Procrustean classification of the factors of production, Soviet theorists have managed to "combine" the sectors of their input-output tables to conform with the Marxian classification.[27] Most Western economists would consider the division of an input-output table into quadrants which show capital inputs and "surplus value" inputs respectively as an unnecessary ideological exercise. But this division has no influence upon the values of technical coefficients, final demand, and total gross output. It was no doubt necessary for Soviet theorists to do this to make input-output politically palatable, while Western economists have not been hampered by even such minor ideological restrictions. The important point is that input-output is a technique which can be applied to a wide range of economic problems independent of economic systems.

[27] Cf. Lange, *op. cit.*, pp. 214–24, and Treml, *op. cit.*, p. 189.

Input-Output Analysis and Economic Development

The versatility of the input-output model was emphasized by Tibor Barna in his introduction to the proceedings of the third international input-output conference: "In 1961, at the Geneva conference the attendance was some 240, with about 100 actively participating in the discussions. And they came from 41 countries; from capitalist and communist countries, from developed and underdeveloped countries alike. They represented an international fraternity of economists and statisticians, trying to talk a common language and trying to learn from each other irrespective of political divisions."[28] Barna's remarks also indicate that the use of the input-output technique is not restricted to advanced, industrialized nations; it has become a major analytic tool in the important field of development economics. As such, the "underdeveloped" nations of the world have exhibited as much interest in input-output analysis as have those with highly complex industrialized economies.

The decline of colonialism and the rise of a host of new independent nations after the end of World War II provided a powerful stimulus to the economics of development. Since they now control their own destinies, the people of these nations seek to raise their standards and planes of living. In this desire they have had assistance from some of the world's developed economies, notably the United States and more recently the U.S.S.R.

The objective of economic development is to move in the direction of greater self-sufficiency. The word *greater* should be emphasized. Complete self-sufficiency would mean sacrificing the benefits of the international division of labor and exchange. But some of the world's underdeveloped nations have relied almost exclusively on imports for most manufactured products. If they are to achieve higher standards of living they must become more self-sufficient than they have been in the past. This implies industrialization, and the latter, in turn, requires imports of capital goods while an effort is made to create "import saving industries

[28]Tibor Barna (ed.), *Structural Interdependence and Economic Development* (New York: St. Martin's Press, 1963), p. 2

in other directions."[29] If the latter goal is to be achieved there must be expansion of "structurally related" industries. In general, this means the development or expansion of industries which produce inputs for other import-saving economic activities.

The process of economic development is not a simple one, and there are wide differences of opinion among economists about the historical causes of differential rates of economic growth among the world's industrialized nations.[30] As a result of the pioneering work of Allen G. B. Fisher and Colin Clark, however, it is evident that the goal of higher real per capita income will be achieved only if there is a shift in employment from primary sectors (such as agriculture, forestry, and fishing) to secondary sectors (manufacturing, mining, and construction), and thence to the trades and services which are lumped together under the heading of "tertiary" activities.[31] Thus economic development means the *restructuring* of an economy, and in an increasing number of underdeveloped countries it has been recognized that this process will be hastened if modern analytical tools are used to show how this restructuring is to be accomplished. It has been recognized that the input-output technique is ideally suited for analysis of the structure of development.[32] As Leontief has noted, the "input-output table is not merely a device for displaying or storing information; it is above all an analytical tool."[33] This is demonstrated by a number of papers in the Proceedings of the Third International Conference on Input-Output Techniques.[34]

[29] Barna, *op. cit.,* p. 6. For a different point of view on this position see the comments by Walter Isard in *Input-Output Analysis: An Appraisal* (Princeton: Princeton University Press, 1955), pp. 366–67.

[30] See for example W. W. Rostow (ed.), *The Economics of Take-Off into Sustained Growth,* Proceedings of a Conference held by the International Economic Association (New York: St. Martin's Press, 1963).

[31] See Allen G. B. Fisher, *The Clash of Progress and Security* (London: Macmillan and Co., Ltd., 1935), and Colin Clark, *The Conditions of Economic Progress* (London: Macmillan and Co., Ltd., 1940).

[32] This is true of the analysis of "underdeveloped" regions as well as of industrialized nations.

[33] Wassily Leontief, "The Structure of Development," *Scientific American,* CCIX, No. 3 (September 1963), 148–66.

[34] See *Structural Interdependence and Economic Development,* especially parts I–III. For a related approach which, however, differs in a number of respects from the basic input-output model, see Leif Johansen, *A Multi-Sectoral Study of Economic Growth* (Amsterdam: North-Holland Publishing Company, 1960).

If a country wishes to industrialize it will try to adopt the structure of an advanced economy. It will try to move from a position of relatively weak interdependence to strong internal interdependence: "The process of development consists essentially in the installation and building of an approximation of the system embodied in the advanced economies of the U.S. and Western Europe and, more recently, of the U.S.S.R. – with due allowance for limitations imposed by the local mix of resources and the availability of technology to exploit them."[35] Input-output analysis provides a map for this process of development. Comparison of the structural relationships in an underdeveloped economy with those of an industrialized economy will show the gaps that have to be filled. And an input-output table will show the effects – direct and indirect – of expanding a given sector or of adding new sectors to those already represented in the underdeveloped economy.

Comparison of input-output tables for two or more economies (national or regional) is facilitated if the tables are standardized – if the rows and columns are arranged in a logical scheme rather than in the sequence prescribed by the official arrangement of statistics in various countries. This is accomplished by "triangularizing" the input-output tables to be compared.

Triangularized Input-Output Tables

The example of a triangularized input-output table to be discussed in this section is greatly simplified; it has been "precooked" in order to demonstrate certain principles.[36] Triangularizing a real input-output table is a difficult task. It is not enough to arrange the rows and columns on the basis of zero and nonzero entries. The magnitude of the latter must also be taken into account, and the arrangement must follow some set of predetermined criteria.

[35] Leontief, *op. cit.*, p. 159.

[36] For an example of the triangularized input-output table for an actual economy (that of Israel) see Leontief, *op. cit.*, pp. 152–53; a graphical comparison of triangularized input-output tables for the United States and the OEEC nations of Western Europe is given on pp. 150–51.

Table 5-1 is a hypothetical matrix of the processing sectors of an underdeveloped economy. The only difference between Table 5-1 and the processing sectors of Table 2-1 is that there were relatively few zero entries in the latter while almost half of the entries in Table 5-1 are zeros.

TABLE 5-1

**Hypothetical Matrix of Processing Sectors
for an Underdeveloped Economy**

Industry Purchasing

		A	B	C	D	E	F	Final Demand	Total Gross Output	Final Demand as Per Cent of Total Gross Output
Industry Producing	A	5	2	0	4	0	3	15	29	52%
	B	0	2	0	0	0	0	20	22	91
	C	1	6	4	2	5	3	16	37	43
	D	0	1	0	2	0	6	13	22	59
	E	3	4	0	1	7	2	14	31	45
	F	0	3	0	0	0	4	13	20	65

Table 5-1 illustrates "weak structural interdependence" as opposed to the strong interdependence illustrated by Table 2-1. We assume that this table was constructed on the basis of Standard Industrial Classifications followed by statisticians in the underdeveloped economy. The arrangement of sectors is based entirely on the customary way in which statistical data are ordered, and Table 5-1 shows no particular pattern of either dependence or independence among industries. It is however possible to rearrange the random distributions of this table into an order which has meaning. This has been done in Table 5-2. which is a triangularized version of Table 5-1. Two criteria were used in rearranging the hypothetical transactions table: (1) The sector with the largest number of zero output entries was placed at the top of the table, while each row below this has a smaller number of zero entries, and (2) the rows have been arranged so that final demand as a percentage of total gross output declines as one reads down the table.

TABLE 5–2
Hypothetical Underdeveloped Matrix Triangularized

Industry Purchasing

		B	F	D	A	E	C	Final Demand	Total Gross Output	Final Demand as Per Cent of Total Gross Output
Industry Producing	B	2	0	0	0	0	0	20	22	91%
	F	3	4	0	0	0	0	13	20	65
	D	1	6	2	0	0	0	13	22	59
	A	2	3	4	5	0	0	15	29	52
	E	4	2	1	3	7	0	14	31	45
	C	6	3	2	1	5	4	16	37	43

An actual triangularized input-output table would not have the perfect symmetry of Table 5–2. The hypothetical table has been made symmetrical to illustrate the principles involved in standardizing input-output tables, and some of the reasons for doing so. Industry B is highly dependent upon other industries in the hypothetical underdeveloped economy for its inputs. But it sells nothing to other industries; its total output goes to final demand (including export sales). There are some intraindustry transactions, but these are the only sales within the processing sector.[37]

[37] The details of the final demand and payment sectors in this table would be no different from those of Table 2–1, and they have been omitted here to simplify the exposition. It should be remembered, however, that among the purchases not shown in Tables 5–1 and 5–2 are those from other countries.

At the other extreme, industry C buys nothing from other industries in the processing sector. More than half of its total gross
output is sold to other processing sector industries, however, and
only 43 per cent goes to final demand (including export sales).
Thus industry B is an example of strong interdependence on the
input side and industry C an example of strong interdependence
on the output side. The table as a whole, however, shows relatively weak structural interdependence.[38]

After the transactions table has been triangularized, technical
coefficients, and direct and indirect requirements per dollar of
final demand, are computed following the steps outlined in Chapter 2. The results of these computations for the hypothetical
underdeveloped economy are given in Tables 5–3 and 5–4.

TABLE 5-3
Input Coefficient Table
Direct Purchases Per Dollar of Output,
Hypothetical Triangularized Matrix

Industries Purchasing

		B	F	D	A	E	C
Industries Producing	B	9c	0	0	0	0	0
	F	14c	2c	0	0	0	0
	D	5c	30c	9c	0	0	0
	A	9c	15c	18c	17c	0	0
	E	18c	10c	5c	10c	23c	0
	C	27c	15c	9c	3c	16c	11c

Table 5–4 differs in one important respect from its earlier counterpart, Table 2–3. The latter is a *transposed* inverse matrix

---

[38] In reading a triangularized input-output table it is useful to recall that the
industries below any given row (say row D in the example used here) are that
industry's suppliers while the industries above that row are its customers. Cf.
Leontief, *op. cit.*, p. 153.

while Table 5–4 has not been transposed. It is convenient when possible to transpose an inverted input-output matrix which then shows the production required from each industry at the top per dollar of deliveries to final demand by each industry at the left. It is not essential that this be done although it does make the inverted table easier to read. Table 5–4 was not transposed since this would have shifted the zeros below the diagonal and this might have been confusing. The notes directly below Table 2–3 and Table 5–4 show how each is to be read.

TABLE 5–4
Direct and Indirect Requirements
Per Dollar of Final Demand

	B	F	D	A	E	C
B	1.10	0	0	0	0	0
F	.19	1.25	0	0	0	0
D	.12	.41	1.10	0	0	0
A	.18	.32	.24	1.21	0	0
E	.31	.23	.10	.16	1.29	0
C	.44	.31	.14	.08	.23	1.12

Each entry shows total dollar production directly and indirectly required from industry at left per dollar of deliveries to final demand by industry at top.

As noted in Chapter 3, the inverted Leontief matrix, or table of direct and indirect requirements per dollar of final demand, can be used to forecast the *total* impact on an economy of changes in final demand in one or more sectors. In the following example we will show how such a table can be used for development purposes. To do this we will assume the following changes in final demand for each of the industries in the hypothetical underdeveloped economy.

Assumed Changes in Final Demand

	Original Final Demand	Projected Final Demand	Per Cent Change
B	20	24	20%
F	13	17	31
D	13	20	54
A	15	18	20
E	14	17	21
C	16	19	19

Given these changes in final demand we can (as in Chapter 3) project all changes which will take place within the processing sectors of the table. Such projections for the triangularized matrix are given in Table 5–5.

TABLE 5–5
Projected Processing Sectors
with Assumed Changes In Final Demand

	B	F	D	A	E	C	Projected Final Demand	Projected Total Gross Output
B	2.4 (2)	0	0	0	0	0	24 (20)	26.4 (22)
F	3.6 (3)	5.15 (4)	0	0	0	0	17 (13)	25.75 (20)
D	1.2 (1)	7.725 (6)	2.892 (2)	0	0	0	20 (13)	31.82 (22)
A	2.4 (2)	3.862 (3)	5.785 (4)	6.26 (5)	0	0	18 (15)	36.31 (29)
E	4.8 (4)	2.575 (2)	1.446 (1)	3.756 (3)	8.627 (7)	0	17 (14)	38.20 (31)
C	7.2 (6)	3.862 (3)	2.892 (2)	1.252 (1)	6.162 (5)	4.893 (4)	19 (16)	45.26 (37)

The original transactions table processing sectors, final demands, and total gross outputs are given in parentheses.

We have assumed that the final demand for industry B's products goes up 20 per cent, or in absolute terms (expressed in U.S. currency) four billion dollars. What effect does this have upon production in the other industries represented in the hypothetical transactions table? Reading down column B and adding the differences between the *original* and *projected* transactions, we find that total sales to industry B (including intraindustry transactions) go up 3.6 billion dollars. The increase in transactions within the processing sector is only slightly less than the total increase in final demand. By way of contrast, industry C's final demand is assumed to change by three billion dollars, but since this industry relies only on intraindustry transactions, the total impact upon the processing sector is limited to about .9 billion dollars. The remaining additional inputs needed to satisfy the increase in final demand of three billion dollars came from outside the processing sector — in an actual underdeveloped economy a substantial fraction of these additional inputs would have to be imported. The development implications of this example are clear. If industries B, F, and D in the hypothetical economy could be expanded by stimulating the export demand for their products, industries A, E, and C would also expand as a result of the increased demand for their outputs. In planning for future development, industries similar to our hypothetical industry B would be encouraged to develop in this country. The chain reactions set off by the growth of such industries would generate expansion in other sectors of the economy. Industries like our hypothetical industry B are strongly interdependent on the input side, and such industries therefore have a high "multiplier effect" upon the rest of the economy when the demand for their products is increased.

Since the input-output table shows only the internal structure of the underdeveloped economy, the following question might be asked: How would the leaders of the underdeveloped nation know what new industries should be added to the present economy? The answer to this question would be obtained by an examination of a similar table for an industrialized economy. Comparison of the two triangularized tables would show which new industries would draw upon the output of existing industries and sectors in the underdeveloped economy. By reference to a table for an industrialized economy policy-makers in an underdeveloped economy could estimate the total impact on their own economy of the growth of specific new industries. It would even be possible to insert in the input-output table of the underdeveloped economy rows and columns borrowed from the tables of industrialized economies. Projections would then show the total impact of the growth of the new industries represented by these rows and columns on the underdeveloped economy.[39] Another type of analysis can also be made to illustrate graphically the use of input-output techniques in the study of economic development.

The "Self-Sufficiency" Chart

As indicated earlier, total self-sufficiency is not the goal of economic development, but *greater* self-sufficiency is. The effects of increasing self-sufficiency can be illustrated by reference to what has been called a self-sufficiency or "skyline" chart. Two hypothetical skyline or development charts are illustrated by Chart 5–1. It should be noted that these hypothetical charts are not at all realistic. They have been deliberately kept simple to facilitate description. Examples of actual skyline charts for the United States, Israel, Egypt, and Peru are given by Leontief in his September 1963 *Scientific American* article.[40] The actual charts, which are quite detailed, show the striking differences in structure between a highly industrialized and three underdeveloped economies.

The principles involved in constructing such charts are fairly simple, although a tremendous amount of detailed analysis lies behind an actual skyline chart. The vertical scale of the chart shows the per cent of self-sufficiency. The horizontal axis measures output expressed in units of the country's currency. The width of each bar in the chart shows the relative importance of each of the sectors in the economy as a whole. The area of each bar up to the 100 per cent line shows the amount of production that would be required from each sector to satisfy the direct *and*

[39] This would be done by constructing a new table of technical coefficients similar to Table 5–3 using selected coefficients from an industrialized economy for the "dummy" rows and columns.

[40] Pp. 162–63.

indirect demands of the domestic economy if it were to achieve self-sufficiency. Added to the top of each bar is a crosshatched block which represents the direct and indirect requirements from that sector needed to produce its *exports* entirely from domestic resources. A crosshatched block (with lines running in the opposite direction) is then subtracted from this total. The latter shows the amount of production that would be required from this sector, directly and indirectly, to produce goods that are now imported. The heavy black line, which suggests the appearance of a skyline on the horizon, represents the actual total output of each of the sectors on the chart.

In the hypothetical charts (Chart 5–1) the industrialized economy has a surplus of "direct and indirect exports" while the underdeveloped economy has an export deficiency which is more than offset by the "direct and indirect imports." Although these charts are not based on actual data they accurately represent the situation as it exists today between an industrialized nation such as the United States and any one of the world's underdeveloped economies. Part of the surplus exports from the industrialized economy go to the underdeveloped economy, and many of these exports are designed to increase the "self-sufficiency" of the latter. As capital goods are imported by the underdeveloped economy and its internal structural interdependence is increased, its skyline chart should tend to look more like that of the industrialized economy. Indeed, one useful application of this technique is to project the changes in structure which will occur as families of structurally related industries grow in a country.[41]

It has been noted that the input-output technique can be used for regional as well as national development purposes. A recent study by the Mississippi Industrial and Technological Research Commission illustrates the regional application of the techniques discussed above in connection with underdeveloped nations.[42] Carden and Whittington have constructed input-output tables for the state of Mississippi, using 1961 data, and from these they have derived a skyline or self-sufficiency chart. On the

[41] For an example of a projected skyline chart superimposed on an actual chart (for Peru) see Leontief, *op. cit.,* p. 164.

[42] John G. D. Carden and F. B. Whittington, Jr., *Studies in the Economic Structure of the State of Mississippi,* I (Jackson, Miss.: Mississippi Industrial and Technological Research Commission, 1964).

CHART 5-1

Hypothetical "Skyline" Development Charts

Industrialized Economy

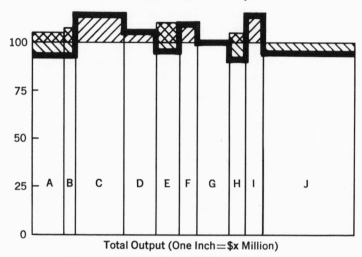

Per Cent of Self-Sufficiency

Total Output (One Inch＝$x Million)

Underdeveloped Economy

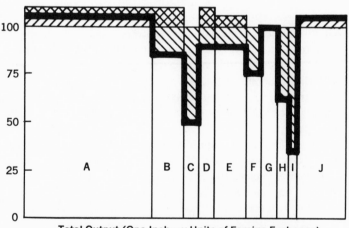

Total Output (One Inch＝y Units of Foreign Exchange)

A—Agriculture
B—Mining
C—Manufacturing (Heavy Durables)
D—Manufacturing (Light Durables)
E—Manufacturing (Non-Durables)

F—Construction
G—Trade
H—Transportation
I—Finance
J—Services

 Direct and Indirect Exports   Direct and Indirect Imports

Actual Output

basis of their analysis they have identified a number of structurally related industries which should be encouraged to grow in the state if it is to optimize the use of its resources and significantly increase its per capita income. As in the case of national development programs, these authors do not suggest that Mississippi should become completely self-sufficient. They define self-sufficiency as "the amount of exports which each industry is able to generate to pay for the imports of goods of that industry which the economy does not produce."[43] They recognize fully the benefits of specialization and exchange. There is a great deal of specialization within "industries," however, so that "self-sufficiency" as they have defined it would mean not less but more interregional trade. As in our earlier hypothetical analysis, their study indicates the benefits that would accrue to the state if industries which would derive many of their inputs from other Mississippi sectors could be encouraged to expand in the state.

Conclusions

The input-output method is now being used as a basic analytical tool by government agencies in a large number of countries. While Leontief's original model was applied to a private-enterprise economy – in which changes in final demand are autonomous – it has been used extensively in recent years by countries with centrally planned economic systems. This demonstrates the value-free nature of input-output analysis. It is an analytical tool which is not tied to any particular system of economic decision-making.

The advantage of input-output analysis in the study of economic development is that it shows in detail how changes in one or more sectors of the economy will affect the total economy. No one has claimed that all that is needed is an input-output table (or any other analytical tool) to *achieve* economic growth. Leontief has put the case well: "The mere existence of an elaborate projection will not, of course, bring about economic growth. Much political acumen and drive, much sweat and tears goes into the actual realization even of the best-conceived de-

[43] *Ibid.*, p. 16.

velopmental plan. Progress, however, will be faster along a road well mapped in advance and the cost of progress in terms of labor, capital and human sacrifice considerably less."[44]

REFERENCES

BARNA, TIBOR (ed.), *Structural Interdependence and Economic Development,* Proceedings of an International Conference on Input-Output Techniques. Geneva, September 1961 (New York: St. Martin's Press, 1963).

———, *The Structural Interdependence of the Economy,* Proceedings of an International Conference on Input-Output Analysis, Varenna, June 27–July 10, 1954 (New York and Milan: John Wiley & Sons and A. Giuffre, 1956).

Board of Trade and Central Statistical Office, *Input-Output Tables for the United Kingdom, 1954* (London: Her Majesty's Stationery Office, 1961).

CARDEN, JOHN G. D. and F. B. WHITTINGTON, JR., *Studies in the Economic Structure of the State of Mississippi* (Jackson, Miss.: Mississippi Industrial and Technological Research Commission, 1964).

European Committee for Economic and Social Progress (CEPES), *French and Other National Economic Plans for Growth* (New York: Committee for Economic Development, June 1963).

KANTOROVICH, L. C., "Mathematical Methods of Organizing and Planning Production," *Management Science,* VI (July 1960), 366–422.

LANGE, OSKAR, *Introduction to Econometrics* (2d ed.; New York: The Macmillan Company, Pergamon Press, 1963).

LEONTIEF, WASSILY, "The Decline and Rise of Soviet Economic Science," *Foreign Affairs* 38 (January 1960), 261–72.

———, "The Structure of Development," *Scientific American,* CCIX (September 1963), 148–66.

LEVINE, HERBERT S., "Input-Output Analysis and Soviet Planning," *American Economic Review,* LII (May 1962), 127–37. Comments by James Blackman, pp. 159–62.

TREML, VLADIMIR G., "Economic Interrelations in the Soviet Union," *Annual Economic Indicators for the U.S.S.R.,* Joint Economic Committee (February 1964) (Washington, D.C.: U. S. Government Printing Office, 1964), pp. 185–213.

[44]*Op. cit.,* p. 166.

6 The Frontiers of Input-Output Analysis

The static, open input-output model discussed in preceding chapters is a flexible analytical tool. It can be "opened" or "closed" to varying degrees; the sectors can be highly aggregated or disaggregated, depending upon its purpose; and the model can be applied to local communities, a region, groups of regions, or to a national economy. As it stands, the model is widely used for short-run forecasting, economic planning, and the analysis of economic development.

The spread of input-output analysis has been accompanied by statistical and conceptual refinements. Some of these may be illustrated by comparing the two tables published thus far for the United States. The 50-sector 1947 table, published by the Bureau of Labor Statistics in 1952, was conceptually related to the nation's income and product accounts. But there was a significant statistical discrepancy between the Gross National Product derived from this table and the GNP as measured by the U. S. Department of Commerce. This discrepancy was eliminated in the 86-sector 1958 table, published in 1964 by the Office of Business Economics. The latter table is fully integrated with the national income and product accounts. In addition to interindustry transactions, the 1958 table shows the amounts of income, by type, originating in each of the 86 sectors. These refinements add to the usefulness of the table for market analysis. They will also permit more accurate measurement of the direct and indirect impacts on the economy of major changes in either the public or the private sector.

The relatively short history of input-output economics has been one of continuing research. Much of this research has been centered at the Harvard Economic Research Project.[1] Other economists in this country have conducted input-output research on a smaller scale, however, particularly those who have been involved in the construction of regional and interregional input-output systems. As this is written there is a major effort in the United States to construct a model to be used for long-run forecasting purposes. This effort will be discussed briefly in a later section of this chapter. Finally, as noted in the preceding chapter, there has been a great deal of input-output research in other countries, both those which have free-market economies and those which engage in varying degrees of economic planning. In brief, while the usefulness of the static, open input-output model has been amply demonstrated, even the most ardent devotee of this method would not claim that input-output economics is a fully developed branch of econometrics. In this chapter we will review briefly some of the recent advances in input-output research and touch upon some areas still in the early stages of development.

The static, open model discussed in this book is based upon *current* flows only, and it assumes *fixed* technical coefficients. From the beginning of input-output analysis some economists have been critical of these limitations. Others have criticized the static model because it does not allow for substitution among the factors of production, and some have questioned the practice of aggregating unlike firms, often producing unlike products, into "industries" or "sectors."[2]

Some economists who have expressed skepticism about input-output analysis have based their criticism upon departures from conventional economic theory. The assumption of fixed technical

[1] For the most recent, detailed progress report on this research see Wassily Leontief, *et al., Studies in the Structure of the American Economy* (New York: Oxford University Press, 1953).

[2] For a critical discussion which at the same time recognizes the major contribution of input-output analysis, see Robert Dorfman, "The Nature and Significance of Input-Output," *The Review of Economics and Statistics,* XXXVI (May 1954), 121–33. See also *Input-Output Analysis: An Appraisal,* Studies in Income and Wealth, Vol. 18, National Bureau of Economic Research (Princeton: Princeton University Press, 1955). For a critical review of regional and interregional input-output studies see Charles M. Tiebout, "Regional and Interregional Input-Output Models: An Appraisal," *The Southern Economic Journal,* XXIV (October 1957), 140–47.

coefficients is another way of stating proportionality (or near-proportionality) in the production process. In the jargon of economic theory this is referred to as constant returns to scale.[3] It has been argued that while constant returns to scale might be found in some industries, in others we should expect to observe increasing or decreasing returns to scale. The static input-output model assumes constant returns to scale for all sectors, however, and it is this which has disturbed some critics. As Evans and Hoffenberg have pointed out, however, "the question as to proportionality, linearity or nonlinearity is not properly conceptual, but rather a subject for empirical investigation and an appeal to facts. The point is stressed because the assumption of proportionality and the interindustry relations approach have been sometimes discussed as if they were necessarily related; in fact, they are largely independent."[4]

Few economists have been critical of the input-output technique when it is used for describing the *structure* of an economy at a given time. What the critics have questioned is the usefulness of input-output as a predictive device. Milton Friedman has stated this point of view as follows: " . . . I want to emphasize at the outset the distinction between the input-output *table*, regarded as a statistical description of certain features of the economy, and input-output *analysis*, regarded as a means of predicting the consequences of changes in *circumstances*."[5] But as noted in earlier chapters, input-output techniques have been used for making projections both in the United States and in other countries. How have these projections compared with those made by other methods? Before answering this question a few comments on the general problem of forecasting in a free-market economy are in order.

In unplanned economies *all* forecasts or projections are subject to a certain margin of error. This is partly because of the built-in uncertainties inherent in free-market economic systems. There are many forces in such economic systems affecting both produc-

---

[3] If the proportional change in output is *greater than* the change in all inputs, we have *increasing* returns to scale; if output changes in *smaller* proportions than all inputs we have *decreasing* returns to scale.

[4] W. Duane Evans and Marvin Hoffenberg, "The Interindustry Relations Study for 1947," *The Review of Economics and Statistics*, XXXIV (May 1952), 100.

[5] *Input-Output Analysis: An Appraisal*, p. 170.

tion and consumer demand. Not all of these forces can be measured statistically. And even where statistical measurements are available they are subject to errors of observation and measurement as well as purely *random* disturbances. Given uncertainty and the presence of random forces, economic projections can only be approximate. Obviously, if a forecasting technique is to be useful, the margin of error cannot be too wide. But a further point should also be made. Many forecasting techniques are limited to broad aggregates such as gross national product, total personal income, and total employment. The input-output method is used, however, for making highly detailed projections industry by industry and sector by sector.

A limited number of comparisons have been made of input-output projections and those made by other techniques, notably the multiple-regression method which is often used in making highly aggregated projections. In this comparison the input-output method has come off quite well. Perhaps the most comprehensive tests are those which were made by Michio Hatanaka and reported by Chenery and Clark.[6] Although Hatanaka's tests were based on comparison of projections made by a static input-output model (one with fixed technical coefficients), they "are the first to reveal a margin of superiority (though an uncertain one) for input-output over multiple regression projections."[7] This does not mean, of course, that forecasters using input-output methods can or should rest on their laurels. There is room for improvement in economic forecasting in general. It is significant, however, that input-output projections, which are highly disaggregated, are at least as accurate as those made by other techniques which project only a limited number of variables.

Input-output researchers are well aware of the limitations of static models, and have continued to work on both the statistical and conceptual problems involved. Some of this work will be discussed in the following sections. While much of recent input-output research makes use of advanced mathematical techniques,

---

[6] Hollis B. Chenery and Paul G. Clark, *Interindustry Economics* (New York: John Wiley & Sons, 1959), pp. 173–76. For further discussion of other tests see also pp. 157–73 and 176–78.

[7] *Ibid.*, p. 175.

which will not be discussed here, the major outlines can be presented in nonmathematical language.

Specialized Coefficients

In the basic input-output model the technical input coefficients are expressed in value terms. They show the amount of inputs (in cents) required from each industry and sector to produce a dollar's worth of the output of a given industry (see Table 2–2). It is possible, however, to calculate other types of coefficients for special purposes. Some of these are measured in value terms. Others, however, are expressed as physical quantities per unit of output.

Labor input coefficients. Leontief has noted that "the technical structure of each industry can be described by a series of technical input coefficients—one for each separate cost element."[8] While there might be little occasion to view structural interdependence in terms of each item of cost, the magnitude of labor inputs in many industries suggests that a table of labor input coefficients can be very useful. These coefficients show labor inputs in physical terms (preferably man-hours) per unit of output. The man-hour labor inputs can, of course, be converted to employment. From a table of labor coefficients one can derive the estimated employment effects of any given change in final demand. As with the basic technical coefficients, which are expressed in value terms, labor coefficients show both the *direct* and *indirect* effects upon employment of changes in sales to final demand sectors.[9]

One of the first large-scale applications of input-output in forecasting was by the Bureau of Labor Statistics, which made detailed employment projections to 1950 based upon the 1947 input-output table.[10] More recently, detailed employment projec-

---

[8] Wassily W. Leontief, *The Structure of American Economy, 1919–1939* (New York: Oxford University Press, 1951), p. 144.

[9] For further discussion of labor input coefficients, and their use in projecting employment, see *ibid.,* pp. 144–52.

[10] *Full Employment Patterns, 1950,* U. S. Department of Labor, Bureau of Labor Statistics, Serial No. R. 1868 (Washington: U. S. Government Printing Office, 1947); see especially pp. 29–38.

tions have been made for the state of California based upon a modified input-output model. This study included sectoral employment multipliers and showed the direct, indirect, and induced employment effects of changes in final demand.[11]

The question of the stability of labor input coefficients is bound to come up when these are used for making employment forecasts. In the short run such coefficients can be quite stable in the absence of major changes in product-mix. It is likely, however, that in the long run labor input coefficients will be less stable than the basic technical coefficients. For example, if capital is substituted for labor, the *value* of labor inputs is likely to change less than the physical inputs of labor. This is because as capital is substituted for labor the quality of labor inputs will change. Workers with higher skills and more training will be substituted for unskilled and semiskilled workers as a plant uses increasing quantities of capital relative to labor. Because of different pay rates for different grades of labor, the value of labor inputs will decline less than man-hour labor requirements.[12]

Changes in labor input coefficients will tend to be gradual, and they will also tend to be in the same direction. Hence if such coefficients are to be used in making detailed employment projections they can be adjusted to allow for the effects of technological progress upon labor requirements. In her study of the cotton tex-

[11] W. Lee Hansen, R. Thayne Robson, and Charles M. Tiebout, *Markets for California Products* (Sacramento, Calif.: California Economic Development Agency, 1961); see also W. Lee Hansen and Charles M. Tiebout, "An Intersectoral Flows Analysis of the California Economy," *The Review of Economics and Statistics*, XLV (November 1963), 409–18.

[12] The relative shift of capital inputs, in value and physical terms, is less easy to determine. The initial cost of installing "higher quality" capital, per unit of output, may or may not go up since this depends upon the rate of interest, and the latter is not a simple function of the quality of capital. There is probably a closer relationship between the *operating* cost of capital per unit of output and capital inputs in physical units. If power inputs are used to approximate physical capital inputs, it is possible that capital inputs in value terms will be more stable than the physical capital inputs. The number of kilowatt-hours per unit of output will go up as the quantity of capital is increased, but because of step rates the incremental cost of power will go down. Thus the ratio of output to kilowatt-hour inputs will change more than the ratio of output to the *cost* of power inputs. For a discussion of the use of *power input coefficients* to approximate physical inputs of capital see Anne P. Grosse, "The Technological Structure of the Cotton Textile Industry," in Leontief, *et al., Studies in the Structure of the American Economy,* pp. 400–1.

tile industry, for example, Anne Grosse found that supervisory labor inputs changed little between 1910 and 1936. There were changes in nonsupervisory labor requirements, but these changes followed a fairly stable pattern. This illustrates a case in which labor input coefficients could undoubtedly be projected with a high degree of accuracy if one were interested in using them for making employment projections.[13]

Water-use coefficients. Economics is concerned with the allocation of scarce resources to competing uses. But scarcity is a matter of degree. Some resources are more abundant than others, and there are significant geographic variations in the relative abundance or scarcity of different resources. Water is an example of a resource that is in relatively short supply in many parts of the world. In the arid and semiarid portions of the United States water must be carefully conserved. As the economic development of these regions continues it is likely that the cost of water will rise. In recent years a number of economists have been concerned with the development of models for optimizing the allocation of this relatively scarce resource. Input-output analysis has played an important part in these studies, which have broad social and economic implications. And an interesting example of an input-output coefficient which is expressed in physical terms is that of the *water-use coefficient.* Such coefficients have been computed for California by Lofting and McGauhey.[14] Following a standard input-output analysis of the California economy, Lofting and McGauhey computed water-use coefficients which are expressed in acre-feet per million dollars of output. The water-use coefficients "aid in tracing out interindustry water requirements which are usually obscured when attention is focused on single industry usage."[15] As in the case of other coefficients relating physical inputs to total outputs, water-use coefficients can be used both for structural analysis and for projection purposes. The stability of such coefficients is something which can only be determined empirically. Once patterns of change are

[13] Anne P. Grosse, *loc. cit.*, pp. 392–400; see especially Table 8, p. 393.
[14] E. M. Lofting and P. H. McGauhey, *Economic Evaluation of Water, Part III, An Interindustry Analysis of the California Water Economy,* Contribution No. 67, Water Resources Center (Berkeley: University of California, January 1963).
[15] *Ibid.,* p. 62. See pp. 68–72 for the method of calculating these coefficients.

established, however, it should be possible to project water-use coefficients with reasonable accuracy. Specialized coefficients, such as labor input and water-use coefficients, will undoubtedly play a growing role in many kinds of regional and national input-output studies in the future.

Capital Coefficients[16]

The static model is based upon current flows and current outputs. Capital is involved in this system only as part of final demand; that is, current sales to industries purchasing capital goods are recorded, but the latter are lumped together in a single sector called "Gross Private Capital Formation." This section deals with capital coefficients as a *stock* concept as opposed to the *flows* involved in the basic transactions table of the static input-output model. In the next section we will introduce the concept of a capital flow coefficient.

A capital coefficient is defined as "the quantity of capital required per unit of capacity in an industry."[17] A table of capital coefficients shows capital requirements per unit of capacity by industry of origin for each industry or group of industries in the input-output system. Like the basic technical coefficients, capital coefficients are expressed as ratios. These show the ratio of units of a given type of capital to the *maximum* output of an industry. The proportions of different types of capital employed at a given time are determined by engineering considerations. These proportions will, of course, differ between relatively old and relatively new establishments.

Incremental and average capital coefficients. It is important to distinguish between two types of capital coefficients. For a structural analysis *average* capital coefficients are used. These show the total stock of capital used by any sector distributed among the industries in which this capital originated. They also show the total amount of fixed capital employed per unit of capacity. For a dynamic analysis, however, *incremental* capital coefficients are

---

[16]This section draws heavily upon Robert N. Grosse, "The Structure of Capital," Leontief, *et al., op cit.,* pp. 185–242, and upon Chenery and Clark, *op. cit.,* pp. 149–53.

[17]Grosse, *op. cit.,* p. 185.

required. These coefficients show the ratio of *increments* in capital to *increments* in capacity. If engineering techniques remained constant, average and incremental coefficients would be the same. Because of technological change, however, engineering techniques are not constant, and incremental coefficients – based upon data obtained from relatively new plants – will differ from average capital coefficients. The latter are a composite or average of the ratios of capital to capacity in all of the plants in an industry.

Average capital coefficients are based upon the relationship between the existing stock of capital and existing capacity. They represent the capital structure of an economy at a given time. Incremental capital coefficients, however, might be based upon the "best practice" plants in an industry. These are likely to be newer plants using the latest equipment and most advanced engineering techniques available at a given time. Incremental capital coefficients represent the average capital structure of an industry as it is likely to be at some time in the future. Indeed, in some industries it is possible to develop incremental capital coefficients for plants which are still on the drawing board – coefficients based upon engineering estimates of plants not yet in operation. In an industry undergoing rapid technological change, incremental capital coefficients derived from engineering data may be used as the basis for a dynamic input-output analysis. In any case, the major link between a static and a dynamic input-output model is a table of incremental capital coefficients.

Inventory coefficients. One further type of input-output coefficient will be mentioned before turning to a discussion of dynamic input-output analysis. This is the *inventory coefficient,* which is defined as "an estimate of the total stocks of an input which must be held in the economy per unit of output."[18] The capital coefficients discussed above relate to *fixed* capital only. Inventory coefficients, by contrast, are a measure of *working* capital. While the estimation of inventory coefficients is not at all a simple matter, the concept itself is not a complicated one. The definition of inventories for input-output analysis differs markedly from that used in ordinary accounting procedures, however. Inventory coefficients "are based on stock figures which combine for each kind of commodity the stocks of finished goods held *for*

[18] Robert N. Grosse, *op. cit.,* p. 205.

that industry and the stocks of supplies, raw materials, and goods-in-process held *by* the industry."[19] That is, finished-goods inventories are associated with the *consuming* industry rather than the producing industry. This definition is based on the view that "normal" inventories are dependent upon the *input requirements* of the industry which will eventually use them. Over short periods of time, the "normal" level of inventories is not likely to be affected by technological change. In general, therefore, inventory coefficients are likely to be of the average rather than the incremental variety.

Dynamic Input-Output Analysis

The static input-output model discussed in Chapters 1 through 5 is essentially a finished analytical tool, although there will no doubt continue to be improvements in the statistical implementation of this model. Basically, however, the static model will remain unchanged. As noted in earlier chapters, this model has served and will continue to serve a number of useful purposes. Because it is limited to the flow of current transactions, and because of its fixed technical coefficients, the applicability of the static model is limited to short-run analysis.[20]

In recent years much of the research on input-output analysis (as opposed to the statistical implementation of static models) has been directed toward the development of dynamic models. As indicated in the preceding section, the nexus between static and dynamic models is a table of incremental capital coefficients. In a completely dynamic system, other changes — such as shifts in consumer tastes — must also be taken into account. For an advanced industrial economy, however, the major requirement for a dynamic input-output system is a complete description of the capital structure of the economy to supplement the flow of cur-

---

[19] *Ibid.*, p. 206.

[20] *Short-run* does not refer to any specific time period. In the case of a slowly growing economy in which the underlying technical relationships are changing at a slow rate, the static model can be used to make projections extending over several years. For input-output purposes short-run might be considered any period during which the difference between average and incremental capital coefficients is negligible.

rent transactions. While the theory of dynamic input-output analysis is in an advanced stage of development, the statistical implementation of existing models has proceeded at a much slower rate.[21] The major reason for the lag in empirical work on dynamic input-output analysis is the scarcity of data. It is true that in his impressive work, mentioned above, Robert Grosse has developed capital and inventory coefficients for about 200 industries.[22] But as Leontief has noted, "an exhaustive analytical exploitation of the large sets of empirical capital coefficients thus obtained involves extensive computations which will not be completed for some time to come."[23]

Interesting empirical work on incremental capital coefficients in the tin-can and ball-bearing industries has been conducted by Anne P. Carter, and Per Sevaldson has done extensive research on changing input-output coefficients in the Norwegian cork and woodpulp industries.[24] Meanwhile, Clopper Almon has experimented with a 10-sector dynamic model of the American economy. His model assumes changing flow coefficients, and allows for the substitution of capital for labor. Almon also assumes that consumer demands increase with population growth and changes in the real wage rate. Investment is assumed to increase with output, and also as a result of the substitution of capital for labor. This is a "full-employment" model which assumes that the projected final demands will result in sufficient output to fully employ the available labor force which is determined exogenously; that is, the projection of labor supply is independent of the equations in his system. Almon has tested his model by making short-run

[21] See Wassily Leontief, "Dynamic Analysis," *Studies in the Structure of the American Economy*, pp. 53–90. See also Chenery and Clark, *op. cit.*, pp. 71–79; Richard Stone, *Input-Output and National Accounts*, OEEC (June 1961), pp. 117–30; Anne P. Carter, "Incremental Flow Coefficients for a Dynamic Input-Output Model with Changing Technology," in Tibor Barna (ed.), *Structural Interdependence and Economic Development* (New York: St. Martin's Press, 1963), pp. 277–302; Per Sevaldson, "Changes in Input-Output Coefficients," *idem*, pp. 303–28; Clopper Almon, "Consistent Forecasting in a Dynamic Multi-Sector Model," *The Review of Economics and Statistics*, XLV (May 1963), 148–62; and Almon, "Numerical Solution of a Modified Leontief Dynamic System for Consistent Forecasting or Indicative Planning," *Econometrica*, XXXI (October 1963), 665–78.

[22] *Op. cit.*, pp. 209–42.

[23] *Studies in the Structure of the American Economy*, p. 12.

[24] *Op. cit.*, pp. 288–98, 311–27.

projections and concludes that it "is possible for the model to reflect the technology of the economy well enough to be of practical value in consistent forecasting or indicative planning."[25]

Much of the work on dynamic input-output analysis is experimental, and while there have been encouraging results there are as yet no dynamic counterparts of the full-scale static models which have been in use for many years. An operational dynamic model is the goal of much current research, however, and a major cooperative research program currently in progress is expected to make an important contribution toward its realization.

The U.S. Economic Growth Studies

For several years the U. S. Department of Labor, in cooperation with a number of other government agencies and various private research organizations, has been working on a series of economic growth studies with the objective of making detailed five- and ten-year projections. The projections are to be based on a series of assumptions about the rate and patterns of growth of the American economy. Various statistical and analytic techniques are being employed in making these studies. But the basis of the long-range projections will be "provided by a study of interindustry sales and purchases in the economy, and the projection of these interindustry relationships over the next decade to reflect anticipated changes in technology and, if possible, relative costs. These interindustry relationships can then be used to convert projections of end-product deliveries to estimates of output requirements from each industry, covering intermediate as well as final products."[26]

The 1970 projections will be based upon the 1958 national input-output table. The industry output requirements obtained from the projections will be used to estimate the demand for labor on an industry-by-industry basis. Labor supply will be estimated by a series of interrelated projections of population,

[25] Clopper Almon, "Numerical Solution of a Modified Leontief Dynamic System for Consistent Forecasting or Indicative Planning," p. 676. See also, Almon, "Consistent Forecasting in a Dynamic Multi-Sector Model."

[26] *Economic Growth Studies*, U. S. Department of Labor, Bureau of Labor Statistics, Division of Economic Growth Studies (March 1963).

school enrollment, family formation, and labor force participation rates by age and sex. It is hoped that the resulting employment projections can be presented in considerable occupational detail.

Projections of unit capital requirements will be made to estimate both public and private investment and the accompanying capital stock which will be required by an expanding economy. The effects of anticipated technological change on input requirements will be taken into account. A memorandum issued by the Office of Economic Growth Studies mentions the possibility of using a capital flow matrix to relate total investment demand by purchasing industry to demands on industries producing capital goods.[27]

The economic growth project is policy oriented. It is hoped that the detailed projections will serve as useful guides to public policy-makers and to private investors. Among specific objectives, the economic growth studies are expected to provide:

a. A framework for developing detailed estimates of employment by occupation.

b. The basis for evaluating the effects of long-range government programs on the economy, including public works, the farm program, defense spending, the space program, and urban renewal.

c. The basis for analyzing, in considerable industrial detail, the economic effects of disarmament.

d. A capability for prompt analysis of current problems which involve complex interindustry relationships such as the impact of foreign trade on employment and the effects of expansion of public works programs.

e. A model for conducting sensitivity analyses to identify those sectors of the economy which are most sensitive to changes from one pattern of growth to another.[28]

Some phases of the economic growth project are more advanced than others. Given the vast scope of the project and the volume of work that is yet to be completed, however, it is impossible to estimate when the detailed long-range projections will be ready for publication. While spokesmen for the agencies in-

---

[27] *Research Program of Economic Growth Studies,* Bureau of Labor Statistics, Office of Economic Growth Studies, August 1962 (mimeographed), p. 13.
[28] *Ibid.,* p. 1

volved are understandably reluctant to discuss the details of the studies before their completion, it is evident that significant progress is being made toward the statistical implementation of a dynamic input-output system for the American economy.

A "Dynamic" Regional Input-Output Model

A completely dynamic input-output system will consist of a table of incremental capital coefficients to supplement the table which records the flow of current transactions. Such a system is far more complicated than the static, open model discussed in this book. While there is evidence that progress is being made on the development of such a model for the national economy, one does not exist at the time this is written. In this section a simple "dynamic" model will be described which does not depend upon capital coefficients. It is an adaptation of a static model which was developed to make long-range regional projections. Conceptually it is quite simple. The model is based on the assumption that at any given time some establishments in an industry are more advanced than others, and that the input patterns of the "best practice" firms in an industry can be used to project the *average* input patterns of that industry at some time in the future.

The assumption is made that long-run changes in technical coefficients are due to a combination of changes in relative prices and technological progress, and that these changes will be reflected in the technical coefficients of the "best practice" firms during the base period. It is also assumed that the technical coefficients will be affected by changes in interregional trade patterns, and that some of these changes can be anticipated by analysis of long-run trends. The adjustment of technical coefficients on the basis of long-run trends calls for the exercise of some judgment. But an interregional model which fails to take account of changing patterns of regional imports and exports will not be particularly useful for making long-term projections. The method to be described in the following paragraphs is admittedly a bit "rough and ready," but it is the author's conviction and that of his co-workers that it will result in more accurate long-term projections than mechanical reliance upon a static model.

While the example to be discussed is related to an interregional input-output analysis, the method to be described could be applied (if data were available) on a national basis. All figures used in the discussion are purely hypothetical, but the procedure described is one which was used in making a series of long-term regional projections.[29]

Identifying the "best practice" firms. An industry, however defined, is made up of a collection of firms or establishments. In what follows we assume that the firms comprising an industry produce identical products. While firms are identical on the output side (a simplifying assumption to avoid the aggregation problem) their input patterns are not the same. It is realistic to assume that the firms in an industry will be of different ages. It is also realistic to assume that some of the firms will use older equipment and employ less efficient production processes than others. In brief, the technical coefficients of a static input-output model represents the *average* input patterns of all of the firms in the industry. There will be, however, a considerable amount of dispersion around this average. The objective of this part of the analysis is to identify a sample of firms which are above average in terms of productivity on the assumption that this sub-sample of firms will be representative of the average firm at some time in the future.

There are several ways to measure productivity. One method is to express output in terms of man-hour inputs—the standard measure of labor productivity. It is possible, however, that even among firms producing identical products there will be differences in the ratio of capital to labor inputs. A second measure of productivity often used is one which expresses outputs in terms of combined capital and labor inputs.[30] In the study under discussion both measures were used, but primary reliance was placed upon the latter. The labor productivity measures were used largely as a check on the measures of output per unit of capital

[29]The technique employed was suggested by Professor Leontief. It has been used by the author and his associates in the Colorado River Basin Study to make long-term interindustry projections for each of the sub-basins in the Colorado River Basin.

[30]See for example Solomon Fabricant, *Basic Facts on Productivity Change* (New York: National Bureau of Economic Research, Inc. [Occasional Paper 63], 1959), pp. 3–13.

plus labor inputs.[31] After the productivity ratios for each firm had been computed they were expressed in index-number form with the "average" firm in the sample set equal to 100. The firms were then arrayed in terms of productivity class intervals. This is illustrated by Chart 6–1, where 52 hypothetical firms have been arranged in a frequency distribution according to the productivity class intervals to which they belong. The approximate median (halfway point) of the distribution is indicated by the arrow. The productivity class intervals range along the horizontal axis, the number of firms in each class along the vertical axis.

The distribution is not completely symmetrical, but it is close enough for practical purposes. About two-thirds of the sample firms fall within the range of 90 to 130 per cent of "average" productivity.[32] The firms represented by bars A and B are clearly marginal firms with productivity ratios well below average. Similarly, the firms in the bars labeled G, H, and I are well above average in productivity. The seven firms represented by bars G and H, set off by the bracket along the bottom axis, represent the "best practice" firms in this sample. When the input coefficients of these seven firms are averaged, the results are considered representative of the "average" technical coefficients of the industry at some future time. If a ten-year projection is to be made we are implicitly assuming that the firms in bars G and H are about "ten years ahead" of their competitors in the industry, or that in another decade their *present* input patterns will be the average for the industry.

It will be noted that the firm represented by block I was not included in the sample of "best practice" firms although it clearly has the highest productivity ratio of any firm in the sample. This was done deliberately to illustrate a point. In any industry there will be some firms which do not necessarily use the latest and best equipment or the most efficient production methods, but which nevertheless have unusually high rates of productivity. These are often small, family-owned establishments (in industries where such firms exist) and their high rates of productivity may

---

[31] Complete data on capital inputs were not available, but depreciation allowances in the base year were obtained in the surveys. These figures were used to estimate the "combined capital and labor" inputs.

[32] In a normal distribution this would about equal the mean plus and minus one standard deviation.

be the result of unusual motivation and above-average effort. They do not necessarily follow the best practices in terms of engineering design and production techniques. Such firms are considered atypical in a statistical sense, and their inclusion among the "best practice" firms would distort the projected technical coefficients for the industry.

Computing the projected technical coefficients. The second step is quite a simple one. In our hypothetical example, the input

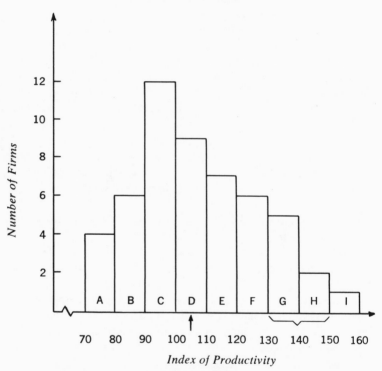

CHART   6-1
**Frequency Distribution of Hypothetical Sample Firms
in Terms of Productivity**

Index of Productivity

NOTE: The arrow represents the approximate median of the distribution; the bracket encloses the "best practice" firms in the sample.

patterns of the seven "best" firms are averaged. From these averages a new set of direct input coefficients is computed by the method described in Chapter 2. From the table of direct coefficients, a new table of direct and indirect requirements per dollar of final demand is computed (see Table 2–3). The remainder of the analysis is identical to that discussed in Chapter 3. Final demand projections are made independently of the input-output table. The new table of direct and indirect requirements per dollar of final demand is then applied to the final demand projections to obtain a table of interindustry transactions (for all processing sector industries) for the target year. If necessary, the changing input patterns can be extrapolated to obtain both an intermediate and a long-range projection. This process is illustrated by Chart 6–2.

The left-hand bar in Chart 6–2 represents the average input pattern of all firms in the industry during the base year. It includes all interindustry transactions (the processing sectors) as well as inputs from the payments sector. In a regional model the latter are important since they include imports of goods and services as well as payments to government.

The middle bar in Chart 6–2 represents the average input patterns of the sub-sample of seven "best" firms operating during the base year. The distribution of inputs represented by this bar is quite different from that given in the left-hand bar. It is assumed that this will be the average pattern of inputs for *all* firms in the industry at some future time. Finally, the right-hand bar represents a long-range projection of the input pattern of this industry. It is based on an extrapolation of the changes from the left-hand bar to the middle bar. This is not a mechanical extrapolation, but one which is based in part upon analysis of various long-run trends.

In our hypothetical example we have assumed that raw material inputs (represented by A) remain unchanged throughout the projection period. The sub-sample of "best" firms uses more inputs from industry B than the average firm in the industry, and it is assumed that there will be an even greater use of inputs from this industry in the future. Industry B, we may assume, provides inputs associated with the increasing use of capital. Industry C in the example may be considered to represent the electric-power

CHART 6-2
Effects of Technological Change in Industry B

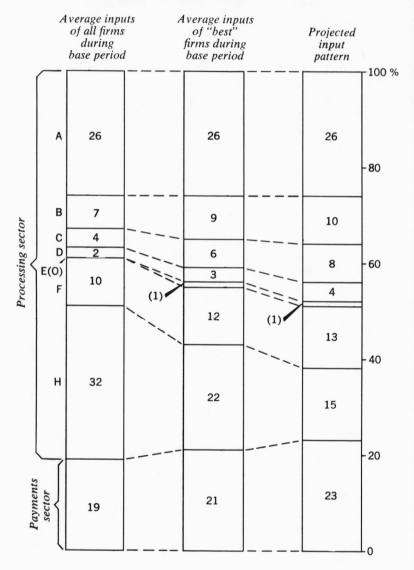

industry. Since the "best" firms in our sample are more capital-intensive than the average, their power requirements per unit of output are higher. Over time, it is assumed that power-input coefficients will continue to increase. There is relatively little change in inputs from industries D and F in the hypothetical example. These, we may assume, are industries which provide services, and while inputs from them will increase in relative importance the changes are not substantial. There will, of course, be some increase in service inputs (notably financial services) as an industry shifts in the direction of greater capital-intensity. Industry E in the example may be considered one based upon the most advanced technology (data-processing services, for example). The average firm in this industry purchased no services from industry E in the base period, but the "best" firms did. And the average firm is expected to use about the same relative amount at the end of the projection period.

The sector represented by H in Chart 6–2 calls for special comment. This is the household sector, which has been moved into the processing portion of the table for this analysis. Labor inputs in the "best" firms are substantially smaller than those of the average firm in the hypothetical industry. On the basis of long-run trends in productivity, it is assumed that labor requirements per unit of output will continue to decline. Finally, moving outside the processing sector, imports into the region and payments to government show a slight relative increase as we move from the left-hand bar to the right-hand bar.

It should be emphasized that the figures used in this illustration are hypothetical. They are not at all unrealistic, however, since the major change illustrated by our example is a shift in the direction of greater capital-intensity. The "best practice" firms in an industry will be those which move ahead of their competitors in terms of engineering design, capital equipment, and production methods. In an industry characterized by rapid technological change, establishments which do not keep abreast of new developments are likely to fall by the wayside. This is part of the process of economic growth, and while nothing can be said about the future of an individual firm or establishment in an industry the "average" input pattern for the industry will change over time. In some industries the changes are rapid and in others they occur slowly. It is essential, however, that the best possible estimates of future input requirements be made when an input-output model is used for making detailed long-term projections of interindustry transactions.

The simple model sketched in the preceding paragraphs lacks the elegance and rigor of a truly dynamic model. The application of this technique in making input-output projections requires a certain amount of judgment. There is no mechanical method, for example, for selecting a sub-sample of "best practice" firms in each industry. If the industry sample includes enough firms, they can be arranged in a distribution such as that illustrated by Chart 6–1. Then the method of selecting the "best practice" firms is rather mechanical. In some cases (utilities, for example) there are only a few firms, and in these cases a combination of judgment and analysis of long-run trends is required to estimate future input patterns. There is also no assurance that input patterns will shift from the average of all firms in the industry to the average of the "best practice" firms over the period covered by the projections. If complete historical data were available on each firm in the sample it might be possible to determine with greater accuracy the length of time required for such a shift to take place. Finally, the aggregation problem has been "assumed away" in our hypothetical example. And in the application of this technique it remains one of the most vexatious problems to be dealt with.

Because of the assumptions which have been made, it would be the sheerest of coincidences if actual shifts in technical coefficients of the type described in the hypothetical example were to take place over a specified time period. It is necessary to emphasize that what results from the application of this method is a set of *projections* rather than predictions, and in a free-market economy projections typically have a margin of error. This will certainly be true of input-output projections based upon the relatively crude method discussed above. In the absence of complete data on the capital structure of industries in the regions involved, however, the alternative would have been to make projections based upon fixed technical coefficients. It is reasonable to suppose that long-range interindustry projections based upon changing technical coefficients—even where some judgment was involved in projecting new average input patterns—will come closer to the mark than those based upon the assumption that input patterns are invariant in the long run.

Conclusions

Input-output analysis has come a long way since the basic ideas were introduced by Professor Leontief in 1936. When he began his study of interindustry relations in the United States in 1931, Leontief stated, "the objective prospects of completing it successfully were anything but bright."[33] In a little over three decades, however, input-output analysis has become one of the most important branches of econometrics. The static, open model is widely used for regional, interregional, and national economic analysis, in planned and unplanned economies, and by nations in all stages of economic development. Input-output economics will not displace other types of analysis. There is ample room for the division of labor among economists. Some will continue to stress the aggregative analysis which is the heritage of John Maynard Keynes. Others will continue in the tradition of Marshall, Chamberlin, and their successors in stressing the economics of the individual firm. The great advantage of input-output analysis is that it covers the wide range between extreme aggregation and complete disaggregation. Another major advantage of input-output is its stress on *interdependence;* it is the only branch of economics which shows empirically how "everything depends upon everything else." It has brought to realization, in an operational form, the grand design of general equilibrium theory which had its roots in the work of François Quesnay and Léon Walras.

The thing to be stressed about input-output *economics* is its dynamic nature. The static, open input-output model is operational as it stands for a wide variety of purposes. It has won international acceptance as an analytical tool which is an important guide to policy-makers in a great many countries. There are of course many problems still facing input-output analysts. There is, for example, the ever-present data problem. The collection

[33] Tibor Barna, "Introduction," *Structural Interdependence and Economic Development,* p. 1.

and processing of data for the construction of a transactions table, at either the regional or the national level, is a time-consuming and expensive process. As more and more input-output studies are completed, however, this problem should diminish in importance. This will be true particularly if "data banks" are established where the raw materials behind input co-efficients can be stored and made generally available. There are other problems associated with industry classification—part of the aggregation problem—which are particularly acute when comparative input-output studies are being made.[34] But there is continued research on these problems, and as more and more countries conform to the United Nations International Standard Industrial Classification these problems can be expected to become less serious. With the advent of high-speed electronic computers, computational problems—much discussed in the early days of input-output analysis—are no longer serious.

Input-output analysis has had and continues to have its critics. This is not at all unusual. Indeed, it would be unfortunate if the situation were otherwise. The advancement of knowledge is accelerated by constructive, scientific criticism. Weaknesses in any system of thought can be better attacked if they are pin-pointed by detailed critical analysis. This is true not only of input-output analysis but of any scientific endeavor, whether in the physical or the social sciences.

There are continuing efforts to improve on static, open input-output models and on the analytical tools, such as sectoral multipliers, derived from them. But the main thrust of input-output research in recent years has been in the direction of dynamic analysis. This is the area where the greatest amount of work remains to be done, and where the truly challenging problems lie. Significant progress has been made in identifying the data needs, and elegant dynamic models have been developed. The rapid progress of the past three decades should continue unabated. Since the frontiers of knowledge are being pushed back at an accelerated rate in all disciplines, major advances in dynamic input-output analysis are to be expected. The policy implications of operational models of this kind for a world in which economic

[34] See for example Shuntaro Shishido, "Problems in the International Standardization of Interindustry Tables," *Journal of the American Statistical Association,* LIX (March 1964), 256–72.

interrelationships are becoming increasingly complex are sufficiently obvious to require no further comment.

REFERENCES

ALMON, CLOPPER, "Consistent Forecasting in a Dynamic Multi-Sector Model," *The Review of Economics and Statistics,* LXV (May 1963), 148–62.

————, "Numerical Solution of a Modified Leontief Dynamic System for Consistent Forecasting or Indicative Planning," *Econometrica,* XXXI (October 1963), 665–78.

————, "Progress Toward a Consistent Forecast of the American Economy in 1970," paper presented at the Conference on National Economic Planning, University of Pittsburgh, March 24–25, 1964 (mimeographed).

BAUMOL, WILLIAM J., "Input-Output Analysis," *Economic Theory and Operations Analysis* (Englewood Cliffs, N.J.: Prentice-Hall, Inc., 1961), pp. 299–310.

CARTER, ANNE P., "Incremental Flow Coefficients for a Dynamic Input-Output Model with Changing Technology," in Tibor Barna (ed.), *Structural Interdependence and Economic Development,* Proceedings of an International Conference on Input-Output Techniques, Geneva, September 1961 (New York: St. Martin's Press, 1963), pp. 276–302.

CHENERY, HOLLIS B. and PAUL G. CLARK, *Interindustry Economics* (New York: John Wiley & Sons, Inc., 1959), pp. 71–80, 157–78.

GROSSE, ROBERT N., "Structure of Capital," in *Studies in the Structure of the American Economy* (New York: Oxford University Press, 1953), pp. 185–242.

LEONTIEF, WASSILY, "Dynamic Analysis," *Studies in the Structure of the American Economy* (New York: Oxford University Press, 1953), pp. 53–90.

————, "Structural Change," *Studies in the Structure of the American Economy* (New York: Oxford University Press, 1953), pp. 17–52.

SEVALDSON, PER, "Changes in Input-Output Coefficients," in Tibor Barna (ed.), *Structural Interdependence and Economic Development* (New York: St. Martin's Press, 1963), pp. 303–28.

SHISHIDO, SHUNTARO, "Problems in the International Standardization of Interindustry Tables," *Journal of the American Statistical Association,* LIX (March 1964), 256–72.

STONE, RICHARD, *Input-Output and National Accounts* (Paris: Organization for European Economic Co-operation, September 1960), pp. 63-72, 117–28.

7 The Rudiments of Input-Output Mathematics

The first six chapters of this volume, which constitute a self-contained unit, describe the input-output system without the use of mathematics. The construction of an input-output model and some of its applications were illustrated by arithmetic examples. With one exception these arithmetic samples were sufficient to demonstrate how an input-output table is put together, and how it can be used for a variety of purposes. In Chapter 2 the concept of an *inverse matrix* was mentioned and a numerical example of an inverted matrix given. As noted in that chapter, the meaning of these terms was deferred until the present chapter. While the *general solution* of an input-output system can be illustrated by a numerical example, the actual process of inverting a matrix can only be illustrated by means of *matrix algebra*.

To round out the exposition of an input-output system two techniques for inverting a matrix will be discussed here. This is the extent to which we will pursue the mathematics of input-output analysis. For this purpose we will need to draw upon some of the more elementary propositions of matrix algebra, and these will be given without proof and without any attempt at either mathematical elegance or rigor.[1] Before turning to a discussion of some of the fundamentals of matrix algebra, some preliminary comments on notation will be helpful, and it will also be necessary to discuss briefly the concept of a *determinant* as a prerequisite to a later discussion of matrix inversion.

[1] For a lucid and compact introduction to matrix algebra see David W. Martin, "Matrices," *International Science and Technology* No. 33 (October 1964), 58–70. While this article deals with the application of matrix algebra to various engineering problems, it also serves as an excellent general introduction to matrices.

The Summation Sign

Matrix algebra deals with systems of equations, and when dealing with a large system of equations it is cumbersome to write out every term each time an equation is used. A compact notation is needed, and this is provided by the summation sign. Some of the elementary rules for using the summation sign are given below:

The symbol for summation is Σ, the Greek upper-case letter *sigma*. It is used to show that addition has taken place. If, for example, there are n observations of a variable x, then

$$(1) \qquad x_1 + x_2 + x_3 + \ldots + x_n = \sum_{i=1}^{n} x_i$$

The index i shows where we start counting, and the letter n where we stop. In this case all items from the first through the nth are added.

It is also possible to use this shorthand notation to symbolize the addition of pairs of observations. For example,

$$(2) \qquad (x_3 + y_3) + (x_4 + y_4) + (x_5 + y_5) = \sum_{i=3}^{5} x_i + \sum_{i=3}^{5} y_i$$

Clearly this could be extended to any number of sets of observations. The index shows that in this case we start counting the third pair of observations and go through the fifth.

A set of products, for example, constants times variables, may be written as:

$$(3) \qquad a_1 x_1 + a_2 x_2 + a_3 x_3 + \ldots + a_6 x_6 = \sum_{i=1}^{6} a_i x_i$$

Note, however, that a set of variables times a *single* constant is written as:

(4) $\quad ax_1 + ax_2 + ax_3 + \ldots + ax_6 = \sum\limits_{i=1}^{6} ax_i \ \text{or} \ a \sum\limits_{i=1}^{6} x_i$

In this case the constant can be taken outside the summation sign since (4) is equivalent to

$$a \ (x_1 + x_2 + x_3 + \ldots + x_6)$$

Consider next the addition of a set of variables *minus* a constant:

(5) $(x_1 - a) + (x_2 - a) + (x_3 - a) + \ldots + (x_n - a) = \sum\limits_{i=1}^{n} \ (x_i - a)$

This may also be written as

$$\sum\limits_{i=1}^{n} x_i - na$$

The summation sign saves both time and space. Because input-output analysis deals with large numbers of variables and equations it is convenient to use this symbol to summarize entire systems of equations and their solutions. In reading equations which contain one or more summation signs, the reader should observe the operations that have been performed *before* the results are summed. An equation which contains a number of summation signs may appear formidable at first glance, but the Σ only indicates that the simplest of arithmetic operations — addition — has taken place. Some simple illustrations of the use of this shorthand symbol in describing an input-output table will be given later in this chapter.

Determinants

The notion of a determinant may be introduced by means of an example. Consider the following system of linear equations in which x and y are the unknowns.

$$a_1 x + b_1 y = c_1$$

$$a_2 x + b_2 y = c_2$$

These equations can be solved by "eliminating" x between them, solving for y, then substituting the value of y in one of the equations and solving for x. The system can also be solved using determinants, however, as illustrated by the following example:

We define the determinant D as $\begin{vmatrix} a_1 & b_1 \\ a_2 & b_2 \end{vmatrix}$, and the solution to the

above equations is given by: $x = \dfrac{\begin{vmatrix} c_1 & b_1 \\ c_2 & b_2 \end{vmatrix}}{\begin{vmatrix} a_1 & b_1 \\ a_2 & b_2 \end{vmatrix}}$, $y = \dfrac{\begin{vmatrix} a_1 & c_1 \\ a_2 & c_2 \end{vmatrix}}{\begin{vmatrix} a_1 & b_1 \\ a_2 & b_2 \end{vmatrix}}$

The *value* of the determinant is given by $D = \begin{vmatrix} a_1 & b_1 \\ a_2 & b_2 \end{vmatrix} = (a_1 b_2 - a_2 b_1)$,

and the values of the expressions in the numerators of x and y are found in the same way. This is illustrated by the following numerical example. Given the equations:

$$3x + 4y = 18$$

$$x + 2y = 8$$

$$D = \begin{vmatrix} 3 & 4 \\ 1 & 2 \end{vmatrix} = [(3)(2) - (1)(4)] = (6 - 4) = 2$$

To solve for the unknowns, substitutions are made as in the general expression above, and the following computations are carried out:

$$x = \frac{\begin{vmatrix} 18 & 4 \\ 8 & 2 \end{vmatrix}}{2} = [(18)(2) - (4)(8)] = \frac{(36 - 32)}{2} = \frac{4}{2} = 2$$

$$y = \frac{\begin{vmatrix} 3 & 18 \\ 1 & 8 \end{vmatrix}}{2} = [(3)\,(8) - (18)\,(1)] = \frac{(24 - 18)}{2} = \frac{6}{2} = 3$$

Insertion of these values in the equations shows that they have been solved.

The determinant described above is of the *second order* since it has two rows and two columns. Determinants of higher order can be formed for the solution of larger systems of equations. They are also used in one of the methods for inverting a matrix to be given in a later section of this chapter. This is the purpose of including a discussion of determinants in this book, and no attempt will be made to give a complete exposition. Further details will be found in most first-year algebra texts. A detailed discussion of the properties of determinants and their use in economic analysis has been given by R. G. D. Allen.[2]

Some Properties of Determinants

A determinant consists of a number of quantities arranged in rows and columns to form a square. If there are four quantities, the determinant will consist of two rows and two columns; if there are nine, it will consist of three rows and three columns. The *order* of a determinant depends upon the number of rows and columns; a second order determinant has two rows and two columns, a third order determinant has three rows and three columns, and so on.

The quantities within the determinant are called its *elements*. These elements may represent numbers, constants, variables, or anything which can take on a single numerical value. The result of *evaluating* the determinants that will be used in this chapter will also be a single number. It will be important to remember this when we turn to a discussion of matrices in a later section.

Determinants of the second and third order are easy to evaluate and to work with. Determinants of higher order become somewhat cumbersome, but everything that has been or will be said about second and third order determinants in this chapter also holds for higher-order determinants.

[2] *Mathematical Analysis for Economists* (London: Macmillan and Co., Ltd., 1949), pp. 472–94.

Minors and Cofactors

The elements of a third or higher-order determinant can be expressed in terms of *minors* and *cofactors*. In defining these terms we will introduce a somewhat different notation of the determinant, as follows:

$$\begin{vmatrix} a_{11} & a_{12} & a_{13} \\ a_{21} & a_{22} & a_{23} \\ a_{31} & a_{32} & a_{33} \end{vmatrix}$$

This notation will be useful in explaining the meaning of minors and cofactors, and also in our later discussion of matrices.

The subscripts in the above determinant identify the row and column of each of its elements. The first number identifies the row, and the second identifies the column. For example, the element a_{23} indicates that it belongs in the second row and third column; the element a_{12} goes in row one and column two.

The minor *of any element* of a third order determinant consists of the second order determinant which remains when the row and column of the *given* element are deleted or ignored. Minors will be indicated by the symbol Δ, which is the upper-case Greek letter *delta*. Appropriate subscripts will indicate the minor of a given element. For example, the minor of element a_{11} will be written as:

$$\Delta_{11} = \begin{vmatrix} a_{22} & a_{23} \\ a_{32} & a_{33} \end{vmatrix},$$

i.e. the rows and columns which remain after row 1 and column 1 are deleted. Similarly, the minor of a_{22} will consist of the elements in the rows and columns remaining after row 2 and column 2 are struck out. It is written as

$$\Delta_{22} = \begin{vmatrix} a_{11} & a_{13} \\ a_{31} & a_{33} \end{vmatrix}$$

The *cofactor* of an element consists of that element's minor with the appropriate *sign* attached. This is where the notation which has been used in this section comes in handy since the sign of the cofactor can be determined from its subscripts. We will use the symbol A to represent cofactors, as distinct from minors. If the sum of the subscripts is an *even* number, such as A_{11}, the cofactor will have a *plus* sign; if the sum of the subscripts is an *odd* number, for example A_{12}, the cofactor will have a *minus* sign. The cofactors of the above determinant may be written as follows:

$$A_{11} = + \begin{vmatrix} a_{22} & a_{23} \\ a_{32} & a_{33} \end{vmatrix}, \ A_{12} = - \begin{vmatrix} a_{21} & a_{23} \\ a_{31} & a_{33} \end{vmatrix}, \ A_{13} = + \begin{vmatrix} a_{21} & a_{22} \\ a_{31} & a_{32} \end{vmatrix},$$

and so on. Each of the cofactors is evaluated as follows:

$$A_{11} = (a_{22} \ a_{33} - a_{23} \ a_{32}), \ A_{12} = - (a_{21} \ a_{33} - a_{23} \ a_{31}), \text{ and}$$

$$A_{13} = (a_{21} \ a_{32} - a_{22} \ a_{31})$$

Only three of the cofactors have been written out above, to illustrate the *rule of signs,* but similar cofactors can be written for each of the nine elements of the third order determinant. When inverting a three-by-three matrix, all nine cofactors are needed. To evaluate a third order determinant by means of expansion, however, only three of the cofactors are needed. Both of these processes will be illustrated later in this chapter when determinants are used to invert a third order matrix.

Matrices

At first glance a matrix resembles a determinant. But there is an important difference. It will be recalled that when a determinant is evaluated the result is a single number. This is not true of a matrix, which is defined as *a rectangular array of numbers.* We will use the symbol $[a_{ij}]$ to indicate a matrix. In this notation, i refers to the *rows* of a matrix and j to the columns. To distinguish the matrix from a determinant we enclose the former in square brackets, and continue the convention of using straight lines to identify a determinant. A third order matrix and a third order determinant will thus be identified as follows:

$$[a_{ij}] = \begin{bmatrix} a_{11} & a_{12} & a_{13} \\ a_{21} & a_{22} & a_{23} \\ a_{31} & a_{32} & a_{33} \end{bmatrix} \qquad D = \begin{vmatrix} a_{11} & a_{12} & a_{13} \\ a_{21} & a_{22} & a_{23} \\ a_{31} & a_{32} & a_{33} \end{vmatrix}$$

Before proceeding to a discussion of the inversion of a matrix, it will be convenient to introduce some definitions and some of the compact notation of matrix algebra. We will also give the rules of matrix algebra needed for an understanding of matrix inversion.

Unlike determinants, a matrix need not be square, i.e. it is not necessary for the number of rows to equal the number of columns. Input-output analysis deals with square matrices, however, and this is the only kind which will be considered in detail in this chapter. One other type of matrix, which has a special name, will be considered since it was used in Chapter 3 and plays an integral part in input-output analysis. A special kind of matrix consists of a *single column* and any number of rows. Such a matrix is referred to as a *column vector*. In Chapter 3, when the several columns in the final demand sector were collapsed into a single column, the result was referred to as a column vector. Similarly, we speak of a *row vector,* which is actually a matrix consisting of a *single row* and any number of columns. Finally, a matrix can consist of a single row and a single column only, i.e. a single *element*. The latter is typically referred to as a scalar. The two types of vectors and a scalar are illustrated below:

$$\begin{bmatrix} a_{11} \\ a_{21} \\ a_{31} \\ \cdot \\ \cdot \\ \cdot \\ a_{nl} \end{bmatrix} \qquad [a_{11} \; a_{12} \; a_{13} \; \ldots \; a_{1n}] \qquad [a_{11}]$$

Column Vector   Row Vector   Scalar

Returning to the notion of a square matrix, this can be written in its most general form as

$$[a_{ij}] = \begin{bmatrix} a_{ll} & \cdots & a_{lj} & \cdots & a_{ln} \\ \cdot & & \cdot & & \cdot \\ \cdot & & \cdot & & \cdot \\ \cdot & & \cdot & & \cdot \\ a_{il} & \cdots & a_{ij} & \cdots & a_{in} \\ \cdot & & \cdot & & \cdot \\ \cdot & & \cdot & & \cdot \\ \cdot & & \cdot & & \cdot \\ a_{ml} & \cdots & a_{mj} & \cdots & a_{mn} \end{bmatrix}$$

To simplify notation it is convenient to use capital letters to represent a complete matrix. Indeed, one of the great advantages of matrix algebra is that we can write complex systems of equations in terms of a single *matrix equation,* and operations can be performed with these matrices as though they were single numbers (which, it is worth repeating, they are not!). For example, if we have the following system of equations:

$$a_{11}\, x_1 + a_{12}\, x_2 + \ldots + a_{1n}\, x_n = h_1$$
$$a_{21}\, x_1 + a_{22}\, x_2 + \ldots + a_{2n}\, x_n = h_2$$
$$\cdot \qquad\qquad\qquad \cdot \qquad\qquad\qquad \cdot$$
$$\cdot \qquad\qquad\qquad \cdot \qquad\qquad\qquad \cdot$$
$$\cdot \qquad\qquad\qquad \cdot \qquad\qquad\qquad \cdot$$
$$a_{n1}\, x_1 + a_{n2}\, x_2 + \ldots + a_{nn}\, x_n = h_n$$

We can express the entire system as a square matrix and two column vectors,

$$\begin{bmatrix} a_{11} & a_{12} & \cdots & a_{1n} \\ a_{21} & a_{22} & \cdots & a_{2n} \\ \cdot & & & \\ \cdot & & & \\ \cdot & & & \\ a_{n1} & a_{n2} & \cdots & a_{nn} \end{bmatrix} \cdot \begin{bmatrix} x_1 \\ x_2 \\ \cdot \\ \cdot \\ \cdot \\ x_n \end{bmatrix} = \begin{bmatrix} h_1 \\ h_2 \\ \cdot \\ \cdot \\ \cdot \\ h_n \end{bmatrix},$$

and this system may then be written as the following matrix equation:

$$Ax = h$$

In this compact notation, A = the square matrix with n^2 coefficients (a_{ij}); x is the column vector of n elements, and h is a second column vector of n elements. In ordinary algebra if A and h were numbers and x an "unknown," the solution of (2) would be $x = h/A$. In matrix algebra if all the coefficients (a_{ij}) of A were known, as well as the elements of the column vector h, we could solve for all the unknown x's by an analogous (but not identical) procedure.

Some Matrix Definitions

We have already defined a square matrix, row and column vectors, and a scalar. As is true of a determinant, the *order* of a square matrix is given by the number of rows (or columns).

The *principal* (or *main) diagonal* of a square matrix consists of the elements running from the upper left to the lower right corners, i.e. all of the elements in which the row subscript is equal to the column subscript.

A square matrix is *nonsingular* if the determinant of that matrix is *not* equal to zero. This is an important property to remember since if a matrix is *singular* (i.e. if its determinant = 0) its inverse cannot be defined.

A matrix which consists of 1's along the main diagonal with all other elements equal to zero is called an *identity* matrix. Such a matrix, which is generally symbolized by *I,* plays essentially the same role in matrix algebra as the number 1 does in ordinary algebra.

Two matrices are *equal* if and only if they are of the same order, and if each element of one is equal to the corresponding element of the other. That is, two matrices are equal if and only if one is a duplicate of the other.

One other definition is required before turning to some of the basic laws of matrix algebra. If the rows and the columns of a matrix are interchanged the result is a *transposed matrix*. We identify the transpose of a given matrix as follows:

$$\text{the transpose of } A = A^{\text{T}} \; {}^{3}$$

For example, if

$$A = \begin{bmatrix} 5 & 1 & 2 \\ 0 & 3 & 1 \\ 4 & 7 & 6 \end{bmatrix}, \quad \text{then } A^{\text{T}} = \begin{bmatrix} 5 & 0 & 4 \\ 1 & 3 & 7 \\ 2 & 1 & 6 \end{bmatrix}$$

Basic Matrix Operations

Matrix addition and subtraction. If two matrices A and B are of the same order, we may define a new matrix C as $A + B$. Matrix addition simply involves the adding of *corresponding elements* in the two matrices A and B to obtain the elements of C. This is illustrated in the following example:

$$A = \begin{bmatrix} 3 & 1 \\ 5 & -2 \end{bmatrix}, \text{ and } B = \begin{bmatrix} 4 & 2 \\ -3 & 6 \end{bmatrix}, \text{ then } C = A + B = \begin{bmatrix} 7 & 3 \\ 2 & 4 \end{bmatrix}$$

We could also have written $C = B + A$ to obtain the same result; that is, the *commutative law of addition* holds (for matrices of the same order), and $A + B = B + A$. While it will not be demonstrated here, the *associative law of addition* also holds, i.e. $(A + B) + C = A + (B + C)$ for matrices of the same order. This is so because in matrix addition *corresponding* elements are added, and the order of addition of these elements does not matter.

Subtraction may be considered as *inverse addition;* that is, if we have the numbers $+5$ and -5, their sum is 0. Thus if A and B are two matrices of the same order, subtraction may be considered as taking the *difference* of A and B. For example, if

$$A = \begin{bmatrix} 5 & 2 \\ 4 & 3 \end{bmatrix}, \text{ and } B = \begin{bmatrix} -3 & 2 \\ 1 & -1 \end{bmatrix}, \text{ then } A - B = \begin{bmatrix} 8 & 0 \\ 3 & 4 \end{bmatrix}$$

[3] If A is inverted and transposed, the result may be written A_{T}^{-1}.

In general, the addition and subtraction of matrices is like the addition and subtraction of ordinary numbers since these operations are performed on the *corresponding elements* of matrices of the same order. As noted above, both the associate and commutative laws hold for matrix addition. This is not true of matrix subtraction, however. The associative law does not hold since, for example, $4 - (5 - 2)$ is *not* the same as $(4 - 5) - 2$. Similarly, the commutative law does not hold since, for example, $3 - 7 = -4$ is not the same as $7 - 3 = 4$. Using the original notation for the *general* elements of two matrices, we may summarize matrix addition and subtraction for matrices of the same order by:

$$A + B = [a_{ij} + b_{ij}], \text{ and}$$
$$A - B = [a_{ij} - b_{ij}]$$

Scalar multiplication may be defined as

$$kA = [ka_{ij}], \text{ that is,}$$

each element of A is multiplied by k. If we have, for example,

$$A = \begin{bmatrix} 2 & 3 \\ -1 & 0 \end{bmatrix}, \text{ and } k = 3, \text{ then } kA = \begin{bmatrix} 6 & 9 \\ -3 & 0 \end{bmatrix}$$

Matrix Multiplication

Matrix multiplication is restricted to matrices which are *conformable*. A matrix A is conformable to another matrix B only when the number of columns of A is equal to the number of rows of B. Then the product AB has the same number of rows as A and the same number of columns as B. It will be convenient, at least initially, to define matrix multiplication using letters instead of numbers. If we have two matrices A and B defined as follows:

$$A = \begin{bmatrix} a_{11} & a_{12} & a_{13} \\ a_{21} & a_{22} & a_{23} \\ a_{31} & a_{32} & a_{33} \end{bmatrix}, \text{ and } B = \begin{bmatrix} b_{11} & b_{12} & b_{13} \\ b_{21} & b_{22} & b_{23} \\ b_{31} & b_{32} & b_{33} \end{bmatrix}, \text{ then } AB \text{ is defined as}$$

$$\begin{bmatrix} (a_{11}b_{11} + a_{12}b_{21} + a_{13}b_{31}) & (a_{11}b_{12} + a_{12}b_{22} + a_{13}b_{32}) & (a_{11}b_{13} + a_{12}b_{23} + a_{13}b_{33}) \\ (a_{21}b_{11} + a_{22}b_{21} + a_{23}b_{31}) & (a_{21}b_{12} + a_{22}b_{22} + a_{23}b_{32}) & (a_{21}b_{13} + a_{22}b_{23} + a_{23}b_{33}) \\ (a_{31}b_{11} + a_{32}b_{21} + a_{33}b_{31}) & (a_{31}b_{12} + a_{32}b_{22} + a_{33}b_{32}) & (a_{31}b_{13} + a_{32}b_{23} + a_{33}b_{33}) \end{bmatrix}$$

Consider now the following numerical example which also gives the rule for multiplying 2×2 matrices:

$$\text{Let } A = \begin{bmatrix} 1 & 3 \\ 2 & 0 \end{bmatrix}, \text{ and } B = \begin{bmatrix} 2 & 4 \\ 1 & 3 \end{bmatrix}, \text{ then}$$

$$AB = \begin{bmatrix} (1\times2 + 3\times1) & (1\times4 + 3\times3) \\ (2\times2 + 0\times1) & (2\times4 + 0\times3) \end{bmatrix} = \begin{bmatrix} 5 & 13 \\ 4 & 8 \end{bmatrix}$$

Notice, however, the result of reversing the order of multiplication.

$$BA = \begin{bmatrix} (2\times1 + 4\times2) & (2\times3 + 4\times0) \\ (1\times1 + 3\times2) & (1\times3 + 3\times0) \end{bmatrix} = \begin{bmatrix} 10 & 6 \\ 7 & 3 \end{bmatrix}$$

The matrix product *BA does not equal* the product *AB*. That is, in general, matrix multiplication *is not commutative.*[4]

The noncommutative nature of matrix multiplication can also be illustrated by multiplying a row *vector* times a column *vector*. If, for example, we have the following row and column vectors:

$$F = [1 \ 2 \ -3] \text{ and } G = \begin{bmatrix} 2 \\ 4 \\ 1 \end{bmatrix}, \text{ then}$$

$$FG = [1 \ 2 \ -3] \begin{bmatrix} 2 \\ 4 \\ 1 \end{bmatrix} = [(1\times2) + (2\times4) - (3\times1)] = 7$$

$$\text{But, } GF = \begin{bmatrix} 2 \\ 4 \\ 1 \end{bmatrix} [1 \ 2 \ -3] = \begin{bmatrix} (2\times1) & (2\times2) & (2\times-3) \\ (4\times1) & (4\times2) & (4\times-3) \\ (1\times1) & (1\times2) & (1\times-3) \end{bmatrix} = \begin{bmatrix} 2 & 4 & -6 \\ 4 & 8 & -12 \\ 1 & 2 & -3 \end{bmatrix}$$

[4] If three matrices, *A, B,* and *C,* are conformable, the associative law of multiplication holds. That is, $A (BC) = (AB) C$. It should be noted, however, that $AB = AC$ does not necessarily imply that $B = C$.

A row vector times a column vector, multiplied in that order, equals a *scalar*. But a column vector times a row vector yields a *matrix*.

The associative law holds in matrix multiplication. That is, if we have three matrices *A, B,* and *C,* then $(AB)C = A(BC)$. But as the above examples have shown, the *order* of matrix multiplication cannot be reversed.

There is one important exception to this generalization. In the next section we will define the *inverse* of a matrix which is symbolized as A^{-1}. The order of multiplication of a matrix times its own inverse does not matter, i.e. $AA^{-1} = A^{-1}A$. In this case it is immaterial whether A or A^{-1} is on the left; in both cases the result is I, the identity matrix. That is:

$$AA^{-1} = A^{-1}A = I$$

Inverting a Matrix

In earlier sections we discussed the concept of a determinant, and the minors and cofactors of a determinant. We also covered matrix addition and subtraction, scalar multiplication, and matrix multiplication. Most of these will now be used in our discussion of matrix inversion, the major goal of this chapter. The inverse of a special kind of matrix, to be discussed later, gives us a *general solution* to the equations in an input-output system.

It will be recalled from our earlier discussion that a matrix A times its inverse A^{-1} equals I, the identity matrix. Thus after a matrix has been inverted it can be multiplied by the original matrix. If the result is a matrix with 1's along the main diagonal and zeros everywhere else we have a check on our procedure and are assured that A^{-1} is indeed the inverse of the original matrix.

The example chosen to illustrate the process of matrix inversion is an extremely simple one. In particular, it has been chosen to give us a determinant with a value of 1. The sole purpose of this is to keep the arithmetic as simple as possible so that attention can be focused on the process of matrix inversion rather than on the computations themselves.

The problem is to find A^{-1} of the matrix

$$A = \begin{bmatrix} 1 & 2 & 3 \\ 1 & 3 & 3 \\ 1 & 2 & 4 \end{bmatrix}$$

The first step is to evaluate the determinant of this matrix by expanding along the cofactors of row 1 as follows:

$$D = \begin{vmatrix} 1 & 2 & 3 \\ 1 & 3 & 3 \\ 1 & 2 & 4 \end{vmatrix} = 1\begin{vmatrix} 3 & 3 \\ 2 & 4 \end{vmatrix} - 2\begin{vmatrix} 1 & 3 \\ 1 & 4 \end{vmatrix} + 3\begin{vmatrix} 1 & 3 \\ 1 & 2 \end{vmatrix} = (12-6) - 2(4-3) + 3(2-3) = 1$$

The value of the determinant, as mentioned above, is unity.

The next step involves identification of *all* the cofactors of the determinant. These are given below:

Cofactors of $D =$

$$A_{11} = \overset{(6)}{\begin{vmatrix} 3 & 3 \\ 2 & 4 \end{vmatrix}}, \quad A_{12} = \overset{(-1)}{-\begin{vmatrix} 1 & 3 \\ 1 & 4 \end{vmatrix}}, \quad A_{13} = \overset{(-1)}{\begin{vmatrix} 1 & 3 \\ 1 & 2 \end{vmatrix}}$$

$$A_{21} = \overset{(-2)}{-\begin{vmatrix} 2 & 3 \\ 2 & 4 \end{vmatrix}}, \quad A_{22} = \overset{(1)}{\begin{vmatrix} 1 & 3 \\ 1 & 4 \end{vmatrix}}, \quad A_{23} = \overset{(0)}{-\begin{vmatrix} 1 & 2 \\ 1 & 2 \end{vmatrix}}$$

$$A_{31} = \overset{(-3)}{\begin{vmatrix} 2 & 3 \\ 3 & 3 \end{vmatrix}}, \quad A_{32} = \overset{(0)}{-\begin{vmatrix} 1 & 3 \\ 1 & 3 \end{vmatrix}}, \quad A_{33} = \overset{(1)}{\begin{vmatrix} 1 & 2 \\ 1 & 3 \end{vmatrix}}$$

The numbers in parentheses above each of the cofactors represent the values of the cofactors with appropriate signs taken into account. The values of the cofactors are then arranged in matrix form, and this matrix is *transposed*. It will be recalled that to transpose a matrix we convert each column into a row (or vice versa). To avoid confusion with a transposed matrix as such, the transposed matrix of cofactors is called the *adjoint matrix*. These steps are illustrated below:

$$\begin{bmatrix} 6 & -1 & -1 \\ -2 & 1 & 0 \\ -3 & 0 & 1 \end{bmatrix} \qquad \begin{bmatrix} 6 & -2 & -3 \\ -1 & 1 & 0 \\ -1 & 0 & 1 \end{bmatrix}$$

Matrix of cofactors   Adjoint matrix

Only one step remains to obtain the inverse of the original matrix. This is to divide *each element* in the adjoint matrix by the value of the original determinant. Since in our example the value of the determinant is 1, the numbers in the adjoint matrix are not changed — it is A^{-1}, the inverted matrix we are seeking. To be sure of this, however, we will multiply the *original* matrix by the inverse matrix. If the result is an identity matrix we are sure there have been no errors in the calculation of A^{-1}. That is, we must find out if

$$A \qquad . \qquad A^{-1} \qquad = \qquad I$$

$$\begin{bmatrix} 1 & 2 & 3 \\ 1 & 3 & 3 \\ 1 & 2 & 4 \end{bmatrix} . \begin{bmatrix} 6 & -2 & -3 \\ -1 & 1 & 0 \\ -1 & 0 & 1 \end{bmatrix} = \begin{bmatrix} 1 & 0 & 0 \\ 0 & 1 & 0 \\ 0 & 0 & 1 \end{bmatrix}$$

The details of the multiplication are given below:

$$\begin{bmatrix} \{(1\times6)+(2\times-1)+(3\times-1)\} & \{(1\times-2)+(2\times1)+(3\times0)\} & \{(1\times-3)+(2\times0)+(3\times1)\} \\ \{(1\times6)+(3\times-1)+(3\times-1)\} & \{(1\times-2)+(3\times1)+(3\times0)\} & \{(1\times-3)+(3\times0)+(3\times1)\} \\ \{(1\times6)+(2\times-1)+(4\times-1)\} & \{(1\times-2)+(2\times1)+(4\times0)\} & \{(1\times-3)+(2\times0)+(4\times1)\} \end{bmatrix}$$

Each of the expressions within the brackets { } will become an element in the matrix which results from this multiplication.

Carrying out the above arithmetic operations we obtain:

$$\begin{bmatrix} 1 & 0 & 0 \\ 0 & 1 & 0 \\ 0 & 0 & 1 \end{bmatrix} = I$$

This is the identity matrix, and it proves that A^{-1} is in fact the inverse of A.

It will be recalled that matrix multiplication is not commutative in general. In this special case, however, the order of multiplication does not matter. We could have reversed the order of multiplication, and the result would have been the identity matrix.

Inverting a Matrix by Means of a Power Series

The inverse of the above matrix is *exact*. The method employed is also straightforward and easy to use for inverting a 3×3 matrix even if the determinant is a positive number larger than 1. All this involves is dividing each element of the transposed matrix of cofactors by the value of the determinant. The method is not an efficient one, however, for inverting a large matrix, say 40×40. The computational procedure followed when a large matrix is inverted by computer is quite complex and will not be illustrated here. Another technique for obtaining the *approximate* inverse of a matrix will be described (but not illustrated) since this technique brings out the "multiplier" effect of expanding an input-output matrix to obtain a table of direct and indirect requirements per dollar of final demand (Table 2–3). This is the method of expansion by power series, and it will be compared with an exact method for obtaining the inverse of a *Leontief input-output matrix*.

The matrix that is inverted to obtain a table of direct and indirect requirements per dollar of final demand is known as the Leontief input-output matrix. It is defined as $(I - A)$, and its inverse is then $(I - A)^{-1}$. In these expressions, I is the *identity* matrix and A is the matrix of *direct* coefficients such as Table 2–2. Thus the table of direct and indirect requirements per dollar of final demand is the transposed inverse of the difference between the identity matrix and a matrix of direct input coefficients. The matrix $(I - A)^{-1}$ can also be approximated by the following expansion:

$$I + A + A^2 + A^3 + \ldots + A^n$$

That is, the table of direct input coefficients is *added to* the identity matrix. This is how we show the initial effect of increasing the output of each industry by one dollar. Then the successive "rounds" of transactions are given by adding the *square* of A to $(I + A)$, and to this result adding A to the third power, and so on until the necessary degree of approximation is achieved.[5] Since all of the initial values in the table of direct coefficients are less than one, each of the matrices consisting of higher powers of A will contain smaller and smaller numbers. As A is carried to successively higher powers the coefficients will get closer and closer to zero. This is another way of saying that at some point the direct and indirect effects of increasing the output of each industry in the input-output model by one dollar will become negligible. In practice, if the A matrix is carried to the twelfth power, a workable approximation of the table of direct and indirect requirements per dollar of final demand will be obtained. Table 7–1 on page 146 shows the *exact* inverse of the Leontief matrix used in Chapters 2 and 3, and in parentheses below each cell entry is the approximation obtained by carrying the A matrix to the twelfth power and adding the result to the identity matrix.

$$\text{Transposed inverse} = (I - A)_T^{-1}$$

$$\text{Power series approximation} = [I + A + A^2 + \ldots + A^{12}]_T \quad {}^{6}$$

All entries here are carried to four places. There is agreement to the first two decimal places in all but four of the cells. And when rounded to the nearest cent, more than two-thirds of the approximations by power series are identical to the entries in Table 2–3. Thus the approximation by power series yields completely workable results.

---

[5] As a consequence of the associative law, powers of the same matrix always commute. Thus the order of multiplication of A and the higher powers of A does not matter.

[6] After the power series approximation was completed the resulting matrix was transposed to make it comparable with Table 2–3. It will be recalled that transposition of the inverse matrix is not an essential part of input-output analysis; it is done to make the table of direct and indirect requirements easier to read.

TABLE 7-1

Transposed Inverse of Leontief Matrix and Approximation by Power Series

	A	B	C	D	E	F
A	1.3787 (1.3767)	.2497 (.2481)	.2810 (.2795)	.4060 (.4040)	.2721 (.2704)	.2276 (.2259)
B	.4496 (.4481)	1.2056 (1.2044)	.1617 (.1606)	.1860 (.1845)	.1194 (.1182)	.2366 (.2354)
C	.2651 (.2631)	.3849 (.3834)	1.3802 (1.3788)	.2329 (.2310)	.1665 (.1649)	.3937 (.3921)
D	.3452 (.3424)	.2523 (.2501)	.2497 (.2477)	1.5293 (1.5266)	.6464 (.6441)	.4057 (.4034)
E	.3542 (.3521)	.2575 (.2559)	.3068 (.3052)	.3862 (.3842)	1.2815 (1.2798)	.2542 (.2524)
F	.3783 (.3763)	.3544 (.3529)	.2239 (.2225)	.2952 (.2933)	.2112 (.2096)	1.3223 (1.3207)

As a practical matter, there is little point in expanding a matrix by means of a power series. With today's high-speed electronic computers and efficient computational methods, it is possible to obtain an exact inverse as rapidly, and at no higher cost, than to estimate the inverse by expansion of a power series. The reason for mentioning the power series approximation is that it conveys more clearly than the mechanical process of inversion the step by step, or incremental, way in which the *indirect* effects of interindustry transactions are propagated throughout the system. Moore and Petersen have also suggested that each of the terms in the power series can be used to represent the interaction between changes in final demand, over time, and the direct and indirect transactions required to satisfy the successive changes in final demand.[7]

[7] Frederick T. Moore and James W. Petersen, "Regional Analysis: An Interindustry Model of Utah," *The Review of Economics and Statistics*, XXXVII (November 1955), 380–81.

A third method of approximating a table of direct and indirect effects will be mentioned, but will not be described here. This is the *iterative* method of computing successive "rounds" of production needed to satisfy a given level of final demand. Like the approximation by power series, this method has the advantage of showing clearly the incremental nature of *indirect* effects. It also shows how the indirect effects converge toward zero as successive "rounds" of transactions are completed.[8]

The Input-Output System — A Symbolic Summary

We are now in position to summarize the static, open input-output system in symbolic language.

Basically, the input-output model is a general theory of production. All components of final demand are considered to be data. The problem is to determine the levels of production in each sector which are required to satisfy the given level of final demand.

The static, open model is based upon three fundamental assumptions. These are that:

1. Each group of commodities is supplied by a single production sector.

2. The inputs to each sector are a unique function of the level of output of that sector.

3. There are no external economies or diseconomies.

The economy consists of $n + 1$ sectors. Of these, one sector — that representing final demand — is autonomous. The remaining n sectors are nonautonomous, and structural interrelationships can be established among them.[9]

Total production in any one sector during the period selected for study may be represented by the symbol X_i. Some of this production will be used to satisfy the requirements of other nonautonomous sectors. The remainder will be consumed by the

[8] A detailed example of the incremental method is given in Hollis B. Chenery and Paul G. Clark, *Interindustry Economics* (New York: John Wiley & Sons, Inc., 1959), pp. 27–31.

[9] Otherwise stated final demand, for each sector, is an *exogenous* variable, and the interindustry transactions are *endogenous* variables.

autonomous sector. This situation may be represented by the following balance equation:

(1) $X_i = X_{i1} + X_{i2} + \ldots + X_{in} + X_f \ (i = 1 \ldots n)$

where X_f is the autonomous sector, and the remaining terms on the right-hand side of the equation are the nonautonomous sectors in the system.

Assumption (2) above states that the demand for part of the output of one nonautonomous sector X_i by another nonautonomous sector X_j is a unique function of the level of production in X_j. That is:

(2) $$X_{ij} = a_{ij} X_j$$

Substituting (2) in equation (1) yields

(3) $X_i = a_{i1} (X_1) + a_{i2} (X_2) + \ldots a_{in}(X_n) + X_f \ (i = 1 \ldots n)$

This may be written more compactly as

(4) $$X_i = \sum_{j=1}^{n} a_{ij} (X_j) + X_f \ \ (i = 1 \ldots n)$$

where X_j is the amount demanded by the jth sector from the ith sector, and X_f represents the end-product (final) demand for the output of this sector. The model can be illustrated schematically in Figure 7-1.

From the transactions table (Table 2–1) the *technical coefficients* are computed (Table 2–2). These coefficients show the direct purchases by each sector from every other sector per dollar of output. They are given in equation (2) above, which may be rewritten as:

(5) $$a_{ij} = \frac{X_{ij}}{X_j}$$

The coefficients are computed for the processing sector only in two steps:

FIGURE 7–1

**Schematic Representation of the Transactions Table
of a Static, Open Input-Output Model**

Industry Purchasing → ⟍ Industry Producing ↓		X_f	X_i
	Processing Sectors $\displaystyle\sum_{j=1}^{n} a_{ij}\ (X_j)$ Processing Sectors	Final Demand	Total Gross Output
$X_p \equiv X_f$	Payments Sectors		
$X_o \equiv X_i$	Total Gross Outlays		

(1) Inventory depletion during the base period is subtracted from total gross output to obtain adjusted *gross* output.

(2) The entry in each column of the processing sector is divided by adjusted gross output to obtain the a_{ij} shown in (5). This gives the following matrix of technical coefficients.

$$(6) \qquad A = \begin{bmatrix} a_{ll} & \cdots & a_{lj} & \cdots & a_{ln} \\ \cdot & & \cdot & & \cdot \\ \cdot & & \cdot & & \cdot \\ \cdot & & \cdot & & \cdot \\ a_{il} & \cdots & a_{ij} & \cdots & a_{in} \\ \cdot & & \cdot & & \cdot \\ \cdot & & \cdot & & \cdot \\ \cdot & & \cdot & & \cdot \\ a_{nl} & \cdots & a_{nj} & \cdots & a_{nn} \end{bmatrix}$$

As noted in the preceding section, the table of direct and indirect requirements per dollar of final demand is obtained by inverting a Leontief matrix, which is defined as $(I - A)$. The new matrix of coefficients showing direct and indirect effects (Table 2–3) is generally transposed to obtain $(I - A)_T^{-1}$. This matrix may be designated as R.

$$(7) \qquad R = \begin{bmatrix} r_{ll} & \cdots & r_{lj} & \cdots & r_{ln} \\ \cdot & & \cdot & & \cdot \\ \cdot & & \cdot & & \cdot \\ \cdot & & \cdot & & \cdot \\ r_{il} & \cdots & r_{ij} & \cdots & r_{in} \\ \cdot & & \cdot & & \cdot \\ \cdot & & \cdot & & \cdot \\ \cdot & & \cdot & & \cdot \\ r_{nl} & \cdots & r_{nj} & \cdots & r_{nn} \end{bmatrix}$$

Analytically, the input-output problem is that of determining the interindustry transactions which are required to sustain a given level of final demand. After a transactions table has been constructed, we can compute the A and $(I - A)_T^{-1}$ matrices. For any *new* final demand vector inserted into the system, we use these to compute a new table of interindustry transactions as follows:

$$(8) \qquad \sum_{j=1}^{n} X_{fi}\, r_{ij} = X'_i, \text{ then}$$

$$(9) \qquad a_{ij}\, X'_i = T'$$

Equation (8) shows that we multiply each column of $(I-A)_T^{-1}$ by the new final demand associated with the corresponding *row*. Each column is then summed to obtain the new total gross output (X'_i).[10] Finally, in equation (9), each column of the table of *direct* input coefficients is multiplied by the new total gross output (X'_i) for the corresponding row. The result is the new trans-

[10]To simplify the exposition we ignore certain inventory adjustments here which have to be made in practice.

actions Table T′ which can be described by the following new balance equation:

$$(10) \qquad X'_i = \sum_{i=1}^{n} a_{ij} (X'_j) + X'_f, \ (i = 1 \ldots n)$$

When the "dynamic" model discussed in Chapter 6 is used in making long-range projections, the fixed technical coefficients — the a_{ij} of the original A matrix — are replaced by new coefficients computed from a sample of "best practice" establishments in each sector. All of the computational procedures described above remain unchanged, however. This could be symbolized by substituting a'_{ij} for a_{ij} in (10) indicating that all components of the balance equation are changed in the "dynamic" model.

REFERENCES

ALBERT, A. ADRIAN, *Introduction to Algebraic Theories* (Chicago: The University of Chicago Press, 1941).

ALLEN, R. G. D., *Mathematical Analysis for Economists* (London: Macmillan and Company, Ltd., 1949).

AYRES, FRANK, JR., *Theory and Problems of Matrices* (New York: Schaum Publishing Co., 1962).

CHENERY, HOLLIS B. and PAUL G. CLARK, *Interindustry Economics* (New York: John Wiley & Sons, Inc., 1959).

JOHNSTON, J., *Econometric Methods* (New York: McGraw-Hill Book Company, Inc., 1963).

MACDUFFEE, CYRUS COLTON, *Vectors and Matrices,* The Mathematical Association of America (La Salle, Ill.: Open Court Publishing Co., 1943).

MOOD, ALEXANDER M., *Introduction to the Theory of Statistics* (New York: McGraw-Hill Book Company, Inc., 1950).

School Mathematics Study Group, *Introduction to Matrix Algebra,* Unit 23 (New Haven: Yale University Press, 1960).

U. S. Department of Agriculture, *Computational Methods for Handling Systems of Simultaneous Equations,* Agriculture Handbook No. 94, Agricultural Marketing Service (Washington, D.C.: U. S. Government Printing Office, November 1955).

U. S. Department of Commerce, *Basic Theorems in Matrix Theory,* National Bureau of Standards, Applied Mathematics Series 57 (Washington, D.C.: U. S. Government Printing Office, January 1960).

Index

TABLE 2-1

Hypothetical Transactions Table*

Industry Purchasing

	Processing Sector						Final Demand					
Outputs[1] / Inputs[2]	(1) A	(2) B	(3) C	(4) D	(5) E	(6) F	(7) Gross inventory accumulation (+)	(8) Exports to foreign countries	(9) Government purchases	(10) Gross private capital formation	(11) Households	(12) Total Gross Output
(1) Industry A	10	15	1	2	5	6	2	5	1	3	14	64
(2) Industry B	5	4	7	1	3	8	1	6	3	4	17	59
(3) Industry C	7	2	8	1	5	3	2	3	1	3	5	40
(4) Industry D	11	1	2	8	6	4	0	0	1	2	4	39
(5) Industry E	4	0	1	14	3	2	1	2	1	3	9	40
(6) Industry F	2	6	7	6	2	6	2	4	2	1	8	46
(7) Gross inventory depletion (−)	1	2	1	0	2	1		1	0	0	0	8
(8) Imports	2	1	3	0	3	2		0	0	0	2	13
(9) Payments to government	2	3	2	2	1	2	3	2	1	2	12	32
(10) Depreciation allowances	1	2	1	0	1	0		0	0	0	0	5
(11) Households	19	23	7	5	9	12	1	0	8	0	1	85
(12) Total Gross Outlays	64	59	40	39	40	46	12	23	18	18	72	431

Industry Producing — Processing Sector / Payments Sector

[1]Sales to industries and sectors along the top of the table from the industry listed in each row at the left of the table.
[2]Purchases from industries and sectors at the left of the table by the industry listed at the top of each column.

TABLE 2-2

Input Coefficient Table*

Direct Purchases per Dollar of Output

Industries Purchasing

<table>
<tr><td rowspan="7" style="writing-mode: vertical-lr">Industries Producing</td><td></td><td>A</td><td>B</td><td>C</td><td>D</td><td>E</td><td>F</td></tr>
<tr><td>A</td><td>16c</td><td>26c</td><td>3c</td><td>5c</td><td>13c</td><td>13c</td></tr>
<tr><td>B</td><td>8c</td><td>7c</td><td>18c</td><td>3c</td><td>8c</td><td>18c</td></tr>
<tr><td>C</td><td>11c</td><td>4c</td><td>21c</td><td>3c</td><td>13c</td><td>7c</td></tr>
<tr><td>D</td><td>17c</td><td>2c</td><td>5c</td><td>21c</td><td>16c</td><td>9c</td></tr>
<tr><td>E</td><td>6c</td><td>0</td><td>3c</td><td>36c</td><td>8c</td><td>4c</td></tr>
<tr><td>F</td><td>3c</td><td>11c</td><td>18c</td><td>15c</td><td>5c</td><td>13c</td></tr>
</table>

TABLE 2-3

Direct and Indirect Requirements
per Dollar of Final Demand*

	A	B	C	D	E	F
A	$1.38	.25	.28	.41	.27	.23
B	.45	1.21	.16	.19	.12	.24
C	.27	.38	1.38	.23	.17	.39
D	.35	.25	.25	1.53	.65	.41
E	.35	.26	.31	.39	1.28	.25
F	.38	.35	.22	.30	.21	1.32